Official Product
from Macromedia

Powerful design and development tools require authoritative technical documentation. With the release of Macromedia Studio 8, there is no more authoritative source than the development and writing teams who created the product. Now their official documentation is available to you in printed book form, to help you evaluate the software or to advance your capabilities as you take advantage of the powerful features in this release.

Developing Extensions for Macromedia Flash 8
Learn firsthand how to extend the capabilities of the Web's most popular authoring platform, using JavaScript. Create commands and extensible tools for use in this authoring environment.
0-321-39416-X, $44.99

Using ActionScript 2.0 Components with Macromedia Flash 8
The resource for developers and ActionScript users who want to use components to speed development.
0-321-39539-5, $54.99

Learning Actionscript 2.0 for Macromedia Flash 8
A detailed introduction to coding with ActionScript to add interactivity and produce high-impact Web experiences. Includes extensive reusable code examples.
0-321-39415-1, $49.99

Macromedia Flash 8: A Tutorial Guide
A collection of step-by-step tutorials that teach both beginning and advanced Flash techniques.
0-321-39414-3, $29.99

macromedia®
PRESS
www.macromediapress.com

ActionScript 2.0 Language Reference for Macromedia Flash 8
Dictionary-style reference covers valuable syntax and usage information; detailed descriptions of classes, functions, properties, and events; and code samples for every element in the ActionScript language.
0-321-38404-0, $39.99

Developing Extensions for Macromedia Dreamweaver 8
Extend the capabilities of Dreamweaver 8 using JavaScript. Write your own objects, behavior actions, and commands that affect Dreamweaver 8 documents and the elements within them.
0-321-39540-9, $54.99

Visit www.peachpit.com/MacromediaDocs for details and special promotions on these new books.

macromedia®
FLASH® 8:
a tutorial guide

jay armstrong, jen dehaan

macromedia®
PRESS

Macromedia Flash 8: A Tutorial Guide

Jay Armstrong, Jen deHaan

Macromedia Press books are published by:
Peachpit
1249 Eighth Street
Berkeley, CA 94710
510/524-2178 510/524-2221 (fax)
Find us on the World Wide Web at:
www.peachpit.com   www.macromedia.com

To report errors, please send a note to errata@peachpit.com

ISBN 0-321-39414-3

9 8 7 6 5 4 3 2 1

Printed and bound in the United States of America

Credits

Macromedia

Project Management: Sheila McGinn

Writing: Jay Armstrong, Jen deHaan

Managing Editor: Rosana Francescato

Lead Editor: Lisa Stanziano

Editing: Evelyn Eldridge, Mark Nigara, Lisa Stanziano, Anne Szabla

Production Management: Patrice O'Neill, Kristin Conradi, Yuko Yagi

Media Design and Production: Adam Barnett, Aaron Begley, Paul Benkman. John Francis, Geeta Karmarkar, Masayo Noda, Paul Rangel, Arena Reed, Mario Reynoso

Special thanks to Jody Bleyle, Mary Burger, Lisa Friendly, Stephanie Gowin, Bonnie Loo, Mary Ann Walsh, Erick Vera, the beta testers, and the entire Flash and Flash Player engineering and QA teams.

Macromedia Press

Macromedia Press Editor: Angela C. Kozlowski

Production Editor: Pat Christenson

Product Marketing Manager: Zigi Lowenberg

Cover Design: Charlene Charles Will

Dedication

The Studio 8 Documentation Team recognizes and honors Patrice O'Neill, who inspires all of us with her dedication and commitment.

Contents

Introduction

This part of Flash Help includes several step-by-step tutorials, designed to teach you the fundamentals of Flash. Macromedia recommends that you go through the lessons using the sample files provided. The path to the sample file is provided in each lesson.

By completing these hands-on lessons, you'll learn how to use Flash to add text, graphics, and animation to your Flash applications. Additionally, you'll learn how easy it is to customize your Flash application by using ActionsScript and behaviors.

The lessons are targeted toward beginners to intermediate-level Flash designers and developers who want to get up to speed quickly.

Each lesson focuses on a specific Flash design feature or topic and takes approximately 10–20 minutes to complete, depending on your experience. In these lessons, you learn how to create a Flash document, write ActionScript, work with video and video control behaviors, and add a Flash component.

NOTE | This book is not a comprehensive manual detailing all the features of Macromedia Flash. For in-depth information about using Flash, from within the Flash application, select Flash Help (Help › Flash Help).

CHAPTER 1

Basic Tasks: Create a Document

You're about to experience the power of Macromedia Flash Basic 8 and Macromedia Flash Professional 8. You'll see how, in a few minutes, you can create a compelling web experience that combines video, text, graphics, and media control behaviors.

You can print this tutorial by downloading a PDF version of it from the Macromedia Flash Documentation page at www.macromedia.com/go/fl_documentation.

In this tutorial, you will complete the following tasks:

Before taking this lesson, we recommend that you read *Getting Started with Flash*, to learn about the Flash workspace. To access this guide, select Help > Getting Started with Flash.

Take a tour of the user interface

First, you'll open the starting FLA file that you'll use to complete this lesson. Each lesson includes one start file, and a finished file that demonstrates how the FLA file should appear upon completion of the lessons.

1. To open your start file, in Flash select File > Open and navigate to the file:

   - In Windows, browse to *boot drive*\Program Files\Macromedia\ Flash 8\Samples and Tutorials\Tutorial Assets\Basic Tasks\ Create a Document and double-click document_start.fla.

   - On the Macintosh, browse to *Macintosh HD*/Applications/ Macromedia Flash 8/Samples and Tutorials/Tutorial Assets/ Basic Tasks/Create a Document and double-click document_start.fla.

> **NOTE** The Create a Document folder contains completed versions of the tutorial FLA files for your reference.

The document opens in the Flash authoring environment. The document already includes two layers in the Timeline. To learn more about layers, select Help > Flash Tutorials > Basic Flash > Work with Layers.

One of the layers is named Guides, which contains items to assist you in placing objects correctly on the Stage. The other layer is named Content. This is the layer in which to place the objects that will compose your document.

2. Select File > Save As and save the document with a new name, in the same folder, to preserve the original start file.

As you complete this lesson, remember to save your work frequently.

Select panel sets and arrange panels

The Default Workspace Layout panel set arranges your workspace in a way that facilitates taking lessons. You'll use this layout for all lessons that you take in Flash.

- Select Window > Workspace Layout > Default.

  You can move panels around, and resize them, as follows:

  - You can undock a panel by clicking the upper-left corner of the panel, in the title bar, and dragging the panel to another location in the workspace.

    If the panel snaps against a border, it is docked in a new location (or docked in the same location, if you moved it back). Otherwise, the panel is undocked.

  - You can resize an undocked panel by dragging the lower-right edge out to enlarge the panel.

Use tools to create Flash content

The white rectangular Stage area is where you can arrange objects as you want them to appear in your published file.

> **NOTE** You can open several documents at once and use document tabs, above the Stage, to navigate between them.

The Tools panel, next to the Stage, offers a variety of controls that let you create text and vector art. To learn more about tools in the Tools panel, select Help > Flash Tutorials > Creating Graphics: Draw in Flash and Help > Flash Tutorials > Text: Add Text to a Document.

1. Click the Pencil tool in the Tools panel. Click the Stroke color box in the Tools panel colors area, and select any color except white.

2. Drag around the Stage, without releasing the mouse, to draw a line.

   You've created Flash content. Your finished document will be much more impressive.

Undo changes

Flash can undo a series of changes to your document. You'll undo the artwork that you just created.

1. To see the undo feature in action, first open the History panel (Window > Other Panels > History).

   The Pencil tool appears in the panel, because using the tool was your last action.

2. Do one of the following:
   - Select Edit > Undo Pencil Tool.
   - Press Control+Z (Windows) or Command+Z (Macintosh).

   Your scribbles disappear from the Stage. The History panel now shows a dimmed Pencil tool, which indicates the undo action was executed.

   Flash, by default, is set to undo 100 of your changes, in reverse order of execution. You can change the default setting in Preferences. To change your preferences, see "Setting preferences in Flash" in Flash Help.

3. To close the History panel, click the pop-up menu in the upper-right corner of the panel and select Close Panel.

View the Timeline

Just above the Stage, you see the Timeline and layers. You can create and name layers, and then add content to frames on layers to organize how your Flash content plays as the playhead moves across the frames.

- Move the mouse pointer over the area that separates the Stage from the Timeline. When the resizing handle appears, drag up or down slightly to resize the Timeline as necessary.

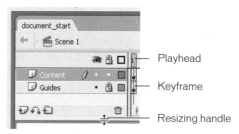

Playhead

Keyframe

Resizing handle

The playhead (the red indicator line) is on Frame 1 in the Timeline. The keyframes are designated by small circles in the frames, which are filled, indicating there's content in those frames. You can add a keyframe to a document when you want the Flash content to change in some way in that frame.

Change background and Stage size

The Stage provides a preview of how your Flash content will appear in your published file. You'll change the size of the Stage to accommodate artwork designed for a larger Stage, and you'll change the background color of the Stage.

1. In the Tools panel, click the Selection tool.

2. On the Stage, click anywhere in the gray workspace that surrounds the Stage, or on the background area of the Stage, so that no objects are selected.

   The Property inspector, under the Stage, displays properties for the document when no objects are selected.

3. To change the Stage background color, click the Background color box and select a light shade of gray, such as gray with the hexadecimal value of #CCCCCC.

4. To change the Stage size, click Size in the Property inspector. In the Document Properties dialog box, enter **750** for the Stage width, and then click OK.

   The Stage resizes to 750 pixels wide.

Change your view of the Stage

You can change your view of the Stage without affecting the actual Stage size of your document.

1. In the Stage View text box, above the right side of the Stage, enter **500%**. Then press Enter (Windows) or Return (Macintosh).

   Your view of the Stage enlarges to 500%.

2. In the Stage View pop-up menu, which you access by clicking the control to the right of the text box, select 100% to view the Stage in dimensions that correspond to the size of the published Flash content.

View the Library panel

Flash content that you import or that is a symbol is stored in your Library panel. To learn more about symbols and instances, select Help > Flash Tutorials > Basic Tasks: Create Symbols and Instances.

- To view the Library panel, select Window > Library.

  We've already imported library items and created symbols for objects that you'll use in this lesson.

> **NOTE**
> Flash also contains a library of buttons that you can use in your document. To view this library, after taking this lesson, select Window > Common Libraries and select the Buttons library.

Add graphics to the Stage

To add library items to your document, you verify that you're adding the object to the correct layer, and then drag the item from the Library panel to the Stage.

1. In the Timeline, click the Content layer name to select that layer. With the Selection tool selected, drag the Title movie clip, which contains a bitmap image and vector graphic, from the Library panel to the Stage and align it on top of the gray bar at the top of the Stage that contains the word Title.

    In Flash, you can work with bitmap images, which describe graphics using pixels, and vector art, which uses mathematical representation to describe art. For more information, see "About vector and bitmap graphics" in Flash Help.

2. With the Content layer still selected, drag the text symbol from the Library panel to Stage, and align it with the Trio ZX2004 text that's already in place as a guide. You can use your keyboard arrow keys to nudge the text into place.

    The title text is actually a graphic created from text.

Add video

The Library panel includes an imported Flash video file (FLV). You'll add the video to your document, and Flash will add the necessary frames to play the video.

To learn more about using video in Flash, see "Working with Video" in Flash Help.

1. Verify that the Content layer is still selected in the Timeline. From the Library panel, drag the ggb_movie_for_trio_new video to the dark gray Video guide on the Stage.

2. A dialog box appears that indicates Flash will add 138 frames to the Timeline for the video. Click Yes.

3. Drag the playhead across the Timeline to view the video.

View object properties

When you add an object to the Stage, you can select it, and then view and change its properties in the Property inspector. The type of object selected determines which properties appear. For example, if you select a text object (not a text graphic, which you use in this lesson), the Property inspector displays settings such as font, type size, and paragraph formatting, which you can either view or change. If no object is selected, the Property inspector displays properties for the entire document.

1. On the Stage, with the Selection tool selected, click the Title graphic.

   The Property inspector (Window > Properties > Properties) shows specifications, such as height, width, and Stage coordinates, for the movie clip.

2. On the Stage, click the bounding box for the video movie clip that you dragged to the Stage and view its attributes in the Property inspector.

3. In the Instance Name text box of the Property inspector, enter **video** as the instance name.

> **NOTE**
> An instance is an occurance of a symbol on the Stage. Because ActionScript, the Flash scripting language, often refers to instance names in order to perform operations on instances, it is a good practice to name the instances you create. To learn more about naming instances, see the tutorial: "ActionScript: Write Scripts" on page 235.

Add video control behaviors

Behaviors let you add complex functionality to your document easily, without having to know ActionScript, the Flash scripting language. You'll now add behaviors for video control.

1. In the Timeline, click Frame 1 of the Content layer to select it, if it's not already selected.

2. On the Stage, click the Play movie clip instance (which looks like a play button) to select it. In the Behaviors panel (Window > Behaviors), click Add (+) and select Embedded Video > Play. To learn more about symbols and instances, select Help > Flash Tutorials > Basic Tasks: Create Symbols and Instances.

3. In the Play Video dialog box, verify that Relative is selected. Select video, which is the instance name that you gave to the video clip, and click OK.

4. On the Stage, click the Pause movie clip instance to select it. In the Behaviors panel, click Add (+) and select Embedded Video > Pause.

 5. In the Pause Video dialog box, again select the video movie clip, and click OK.

6. On the Stage, click the Rewind movie clip instance to select it. In the Behaviors panel, click Add (+) and select Embedded Video > Rewind.

7. In the Rewind Video dialog box, select Video.

8. In the Number of Frames to Step Back text box, enter **20**.

   The Number of Frames to Step Back text box indicates how many frames the playhead should move back when the user clicks the Rewind button.

NOTE
Additional video control behaviors let you fast-forward, hide, and show a video.

Use the Movie Explorer to view the document structure

The Movie Explorer helps you arrange, locate, and edit media. With its hierarchical tree structure, the Movie Explorer provides information about the organization and flow of a document.

1. Select Window > Movie Explorer.

    If necessary, enlarge the Movie Explorer to view the tree structure within the pane.

    The Movie Explorer filtering buttons display or hide information.

2. Click the pop-up menu in the title bar of the Movie Explorer, and select Show Movie Elements and Show Symbol Definitions, if they're not already selected.

3. Configure the filtering buttons, along the top of the Movie Explorer, so the only ones selected are Show Buttons, Movie Clips, and Graphics; Show Action Scripts; and Show Video, Sounds, and Bitmaps.

    If you move your mouse pointer over a button, a tooltip displays the name of the button.

    Examine the list to view some of the assets included in the document, and to see their relationship to other assets.

4. In the Movie Explorer pane, expand Actions for Play to view ActionScript that Flash created when you added the Play video control behavior.

5. To close the Movie Explorer, click its close box.

Test the document

As you author a document, you should save and test it frequently to ensure the Flash content plays as expected. When you test the SWF file, click the video control buttons to see if the video stops, plays, and rewinds as expected.

1. Save the document (File > Save) and select Control > Test Movie.

    The Flash content plays in a SWF file window. Although .fla is the extension for documents in the authoring environment, .swf is the extension for tested, exported, and published Flash content.

2. When you finish viewing the SWF content, close the SWF file window to return to the authoring environment.

Find help

The lessons provide an introduction to Flash, and suggest ways that you can use features to create exactly the kind of document required. For comprehensive information about a feature, procedure, or process described in the lessons, see the Help tab of the Help panel (Help > Flash Help).

Summary

Congratulations on creating a Flash document that includes graphics, a video, and video control behaviors. In a few minutes, you learned how to accomplish the following:

- Tour the user interface
- Dock and undock panels
- Change the background and Stage size
- Change your view of the Stage
- View your document library
- Add graphics to the Stage
- Add video

- View object properties
- Add video control behaviors
- Use the Movie Explorer to view the document structure
- Test the document
- Find help

To learn more about Flash, take another lesson.

CHAPTER 2

Basic Tasks: Creating a banner, Part 1

2

Macromedia Flash Basic 8 or Macromedia Flash Professional 8 can seem like a very complex programs to learn. One reason for this seeming complexity is that you can use it for so many different things, such as cartoon animations, media players, and sophisticated software. This tutorial is suitable for you if you're opening Flash 8 for the first time. This tutorial shows you some of the fundamental aspects of the program, and how to get started using them to build a real project. You don't need to know anything about Flash or animation to complete this tutorial; in fact, you'll discover how easy it is to start using Flash 8 to add elements to your web pages.

This is Part 1 of a three-part tutorial on how to build a simple animated banner in Flash and add it to a web page using Macromedia Dreamweaver. You'll learn how to create a file and modify its settings, import and add graphics to the Stage from the library, and create layers in Part 1. In Part 2 and Part 3, you'll add an animation and create a button that opens a browser window. Then you'll specify publish settings, and add the banner to a web page.

"Basic Tasks: Creating a banner, Part 1" on page 25: You learn how to create and structure the banner application.

"Basic Tasks: Creating a banner, Part 2" on page 43: You learn how to add animation, create a button, and write basic scripts.

"Basic Tasks: Creating a banner, Part 3" on page 63: You learn how to publish your SWF file, and insert the file into a Dreamweaver website.

You do not need any prerequisite knowledge to complete these tutorials.

In Part 1 of this tutorial, you will complete the following tasks:

The tutorial workflow includes the following tasks:

- "Examine the completed FLA file" on page 26 lets you view the completed Flash document.

- "Creating a new document" on page 29 shows you how to create a FLA file that you'll use to create the banner throughout the three parts of this tutorial.

- "Changing document properties" on page 30 shows you how to change the dimensions of your SWF file.

- "Importing graphics" on page 33 shows you how to import assets into your document's library.

- "Introducing layers and the timeline" on page 36 shows you how to create and manipulate layers in the main Timeline.

- "Test the application" on page 40 shows you how to export and test your document's SWF file, which lets you test your progress so far.

Examine the completed FLA file

As you examine the finished version of an application that you'll create, you'll also look at the Flash workspace.

In this section, you will complete the following tasks:

- "Open the authoring document" on page 163
- "Review the completed FLA file" on page 28
- "Close the completed FLA file" on page 28

In subsequent sections you'll go through the steps to create the application yourself starting with a brand new FLA file.

Open the finished FLA file

It's helpful to analyze the completed authoring document, which is a FLA file, to see how the author designed the application. You should examine what kinds of scripts were used to add interactivity, and understand what you are going to create.

The files for this tutorial are located in the Samples and Tutorials folder in the Flash installation folder. For many users, particularly in educational settings, this folder is read-only. Before proceeding with the tutorial, you should copy the entire FlashBanner tutorial folder to the writable location of your choice.

On most computers, you will find the Flash Banner tutorial folder in the following locations:

- In Windows: *boot drive*\Program Files\Macromedia\Flash 8\ Samples and Tutorials\Tutorial Assets\Basic Tasks\FlashBanner\.

- On the Macintosh: *Macintosh HD*/Applications/Macromedia Flash 8/ Samples and Tutorials/Tutorial Assets/Basic Tasks/FlashBanner/.

Copy the FlashBanner folder to another location on your hard disk to which you have access. Inside this folder are three directories for each part of this tutorial: Part1, Part2, and Part3. In the FlashBanner/Part1 folder, you will find a Flash file called banner1_complete.fla. Double-click the file to open it in Flash. You now see the completed tutorial file in the Flash authoring environment.

Review the completed FLA file

In the completed FLA file, you will see the structure that makes up the finished SWF file for Part 1 of this tutorial. The application, a Flash banner for a gnome website, looks like this at the end of Part 1:

The completed banner at the end of Part 1.

By the end of Part 3 of this tutorial, you will add the graphics, animation, and interactivity to the banner. Then, you'll insert the banner on a website using Dreamweaver.

Close the completed FLA file

To close the document, select File > Close.

If you prefer to keep the finished file open as a reference while working with your banner file, be careful not to edit it or save any changes to it.

Now you're ready to start creating your own banner file in the next section, "Creating a new document".

Creating a new document

You can create all kinds of different elements for the web or for CD-ROMs and devices using Flash 8. First, you create a file in the Flash authoring tool, which you use to output SWF files. SWF files are the files that you can put online when you embed it in a web page. The Macromedia Flash Player plug-in then displays the SWF file, so your website visitors can view or interact with the content.

Your SWF file can contain video, MP3 sound, animations, images, data, and so forth. The benefit of using an SWF file over other formats is that the Flash Player plug-in is incredibly common. Let's start building a banner.

1. Open the Flash application.

   By default, Flash displays the Start Page (see the following figure), which enables you to select a recently edited document, create a new Flash document or ActionScript file, or create a new document using a pre-built template. If you use Flash Professional 8, you can create additional kinds of files.

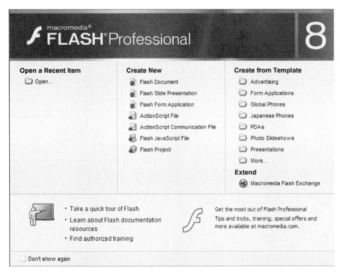

By default, Flash displays the Start Page when it's started. This figure shows the options available in Flash Professional 8.

2. Click Flash Document from the Create New column on the Start Page to create a blank document.

3. Select File > Save As from the main menu.

4. Name the file **banner.fla,** find or create a new directory to save your project in, and click Save when you're done.

   Flash saves editable documents as FLA files. From the FLA file, you export (or compile) SWF files that you can embed in an HTML page. Flash Player, installed on most computers, plays the SWF files that you export from Flash.

After you finish saving the file, proceed to the following exercise, "Changing document properties".

Changing document properties

At this point you're looking at a blank canvas surrounded by many controls (see the next figure). The large white square is called the Stage, and it's where you place assets you want to display in the SWF file, such as images, buttons, text, or animations. The Stage and panels are commonly called the Flash workspace or *authoring environment.* The Flash environment consists of the Stage and a variety of panels, tools, and the Timeline above the Stage. For detailed information on each part of the workspace, see "Take a tour of the user interface" on page 14.

Around the Stage you see a variety of panels. The panel on the left is called the Tools panel (see the following figure). This panel includes tools you can use to create and modify documents, such as tools you use to draw and make selections.

Use the Tools panel to draw and make selections. You use the Selection tool (the black arrow) to make selections in these tutorials.

A panel near the bottom of the Flash application is titled Properties. (Select Window > Properties > Properties if you don't see the panel.) This panel is called the *Property inspector* (see the following figure). This panel lets you change various properties of whatever is currently selected in your document (such as an image or a frame), or set properties for the entire SWF file (such as the frame rate or dimensions). For information on controlling the frame rate of a document, see "Change the frames per second speed" on page 159.

If you don't have any objects or frames selected, the Property inspector allows you to modify properties for the document itself.

1. Open the Property inspector (Window > Properties > Properties) and click the button next to the text that says Size to open the Document Properties dialog box.

NOTE Make sure that you don't have a frame selected. Click the Stage if you do not see the button mentioned in the previous step.

Click this button in the Property inspector to open the Document properties dialog box. You can then change the size and color of the Stage.

The button displays the current dimensions of the FLA file (550 x 400 pixels). By default the Stage size in a new Flash document is 550 pixels wide by 400 pixels high. When you click Size, you open a dialog box where you can change several document-wide properties (such as the Stage dimensions, color, and document frame rate).

2. Type **160** into the Width text box, and **600** into the Height text box.

    When you type new values into these text boxes, you resize the dimensions of your FLA file. You need to use these specific dimensions because you're creating a banner and you should use a standard banner size. In this tutorial, you're creating a "wide skyscraper." For a list of standardized banner sizes, check out the Interactive Advertising Bureau's page on Interactive Marketing Units at www.iab.net/standards/adunits.asp.

NOTE You can also create banners from a Macromedia template by selecting File > New from the main menu. Select the Templates tab and select the Advertising category.

3. Click OK when you finish entering the new dimensions to return to the authoring environment.

   When you return to the authoring environment, notice how the dimensions of your document change. You can also change the current document's background color and frame rate directly in the Property inspector, without going to the Document Properties dialog box. You'll find information about frame rate in Part 2 of this tutorial, "Basic Tasks: Creating a banner, Part 2" on page 43.

4. Select File > Save to save the document before you proceed to the next section ("Importing graphics").

Importing graphics

When you work with Flash, you'll often import assets into a document. Perhaps you have a company logo, or graphics that a designer has provided for your work. You can import a variety of assets into Flash, including sound, video, bitmap images, and other graphic formats (such as PNG, JPEG, AI, and PSD).

Imported graphics are stored in the document's library. The library stores both the assets that you import into the document, and symbols that you create within Flash. A symbol is a vector graphic, button, font, component, or movie clip that you create once and can reuse multiple times.

So you don't have to draw your own graphics in Flash, you can import an image of a pre-drawn gnome from the tutorial source file. Before you proceed, make sure that you save the source files for this tutorial as described in "Open the finished FLA file", and save the images to the same directory as your banner.fla file.

1. Select File > Import > Import to Library to import an image into the current document.

   You'll see the Import dialog box (see the following figure), which enables you to browse to the file you want to import.

   Browse to the folder on your hard disk that contains an image to import into your Flash document.

2. Navigate to the directory where you saved the tutorial's source files, and locate the bitmap image saved in the FlashBanner/Part1 directory.

3. Select the gnome.png image, and click Open (Windows) or Import (Macintosh).

   The image is imported into the document's library.

> **NOTE** You can drag assets from the library onto the Stage several times if you want to see several instances of the artwork. Your file size doesn't increase if you use several instances on the Stage. The SWF file only stores the information of the original symbol or asset from the library, and treats each instance like a duplicate..

4. Select Window > Library to open the Library panel.

   You'll see the image you just imported, gnome.png, in the document's library.

5. Select the imported image in the library and drag it onto the Stage.

   Don't worry about where you put the image on the Stage, because you'll set the coordinates for the image later. When you drag something onto the Stage, you will see it in the SWF file when the file plays.

6. Click the Selection tool, and select the instance on the Stage.

If you look at the Property inspector you'll notice that you can modify the image's width and height, as well as the image's X and Y position on the Stage. When you select an object on the Stage, you can see and modify the current coordinates in the Property inspector (see the following figure).

The X and Y coordinates match the registration point, which is the upper left corner of this movie clip symbol.

7. Type **0** into the X text box, and type **0** into the Y text box.

Typing these values in sets the X and Y coordinates both to 0, as shown in the following figure.

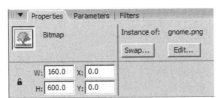

Set the X and Y coordinates using the Property inspector. Set the X and Y values to 0.

Setting new coordinates moves the upper-left corner of the image to the upper-left corner of the Stage. You can drag the bitmap image around the Stage using the Selection tool instead of changing coordinates in the Property inspector. Use the Property inspector when you need to set a specific position for an object, like you did in this step.

8. Select File > Save to save the document before you proceed to the next section ("Introducing layers and the timeline").

<table>
<tr><td>NOTE</td><td>You can also import sound files into your FLA files. This isn't covered in this tutorial, but you can find out more information in "Working with Sound" in Flash Help.</td></tr>
</table>

Introducing layers and the timeline

The Timeline is above the Stage in the Flash workspace. The Timeline, which contains *layers* and *frames*, helps you organize assets in your document, and also controls a document's content over time.

Flash documents can play over a length of time, like movies or sound, which is measured using frames. Layers are like transparencies that stack on top of one another, and each layer can contain images, text, or animations that display on the Stage. You'll learn more about frames and the Timeline in Part 2 of this tutorial, "Basic Tasks: Creating a banner, Part 2" on page 43.

The FLA file you're working on has one layer (Layer 1) with contents on a single frame (Frame 1). This is the default way that a Flash document opens.

In this exercise, you lock and rename Layer 1. Often you'll want to place objects in a particular position on the Stage. To help you keep those objects in place, Flash enables you to lock layers, so you cannot select the items on a layer and accidentally move them.

In this section, you will complete the following tasks:

- "Creating a new layer" on page 38
- "Importing to a layer" on page 39

1. Select Layer 1 in the Timeline and click the dot below the lock icon, as shown in the following figure.

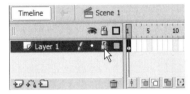

Lock a layer so its contents aren't accidentally moved or deleted from the Stage. You can also prevent inadvertently adding other assets to that layer.

With your only layer locked, you need to add new layers before you can add any other objects to the Stage. You cannot add new objects to a locked layer.

2. Select the Selection tool in the Tools panel, and double-click the name Layer 1.

When you double-click a layer name, you can modify the name of the layer.

3. Type **background** into the layer name to rename the layer. Then save your file.

When you start building projects with many layers, layer names like Layer 1 and Layer 14 don't help you determine what's on that layer. Giving layers a descriptive name is a good practice to adopt.

4. Select File > Save before you proceed to the next exercise ("Creating a new layer").

<table>
<tr><td>NOTE</td><td>You can also organize layers into layer folders. For more information, see "Organize layers in a folder" on page 94.</td></tr>
</table>

Creating a new layer

In just about any Flash project where you use imported graphics and animation, you'll need to create at least a few layers. You need to separate certain elements onto their own layers, particularly when you start to animate objects. You can also stack graphics on top of each other, and even create a sense of depth or overlapping by using multiple layers.

1. Select the background layer on the Timeline, and click Insert Layer to create a new, empty layer.

    The new layer is created above the background layer (see the following figure).

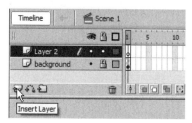

Click Insert Layer to insert a new layer above the currently selected layer.

2. Double-click the name of the new layer so the layer's name becomes editable.

3. Type **animation** to rename the new layer.

    Graphics on the Stage stack according to the layers on the Timeline. For example, anything that you put on the animation layer will appear above the image on the background layer. You will add animation to this second layer in Part 2 of this tutorial.

4. Select File > Save before you proceed to the next exercise ("Importing to a layer").

> **NOTE** If you need to reorganize your layers you can use the Selection tool to select and then drag a layer above or below other layers on the Timeline.

Importing to a layer

In an earlier exercise, "Importing graphics", you imported the gnome.png image directly into the document's library. Then you dragged the image onto a selected layer on the Stage. You can also import assets directly to the Stage instead of into the library. First you need to select the frame into which you want to import the image on the Timeline. Then you can import the image onto that frame, which displays on the Stage. You use this technique to import an image in the following exercise.

1. Select frame 1 of the animation layer.

   You need to import star.png image to the animation layer.

2. Select File > Import > Import to Stage.

   The Open dialog box appears where you can select an image from your hard disk. Find the folder of this tutorial's source files on your hard disk.

3. Select star.png in the tutorial's source files, and click Open (Windows) or Import (Macintosh).

   The image imports to the animation layer (see the following figure), and then it appears on the Stage.

   The image imports to the frame on the layer that you select on the Timeline. You will learn more about the Timeline and layers in Part 2 of this tutorial, "Basic Tasks: Creating a banner, Part 2" on page 43.

4. Open the Library panel (Window > Library).

   The image you just imported to the Stage also appears as an asset in the library. Even if you import an asset directly to the Stage, Flash always stores the assets you import in the library as well.

5. Click the Selection tool in the Tools panel.

Move the star.png file on the Stage to just above the gnome's head in the image, as shown in the following figure.

Move the star.png image just above the gnome's head.

6. Select File > Save to save your document before moving on to "Test the application".

Test the application

To finish, you can test your document using Flash. Doing so tests the SWF file in Flash Player. For example, you can see how your code works in Flash Player, how animations play on the Timeline, test user interactivity, and more. It's much faster than uploading your work to a server each time you want to see the SWF file in action.

1. Select Control > Test Movie from the main menu.

The test environment opens and plays your document in Flash Player. You can now see the compiled SWF file version of your FLA file. You will often use the Test Movie command to view your progress when you work on an FLA file.

2. Click the close button of the window that contains the SWF file to return to the authoring environment.

Find the folder on your hard disk where you saved banner.fla at the beginning of this tutorial in "Creating a new document".

When you open this folder, you should see an additional SWF file called banner.swf. This is the compiled version of the banner.fla file. When you want to create a finished version of your file to upload, you'll want to make additional publish settings in Flash before you compile your SWF file. You'll look at these settings in Part 3 ("Basic Tasks: Creating a banner, Part 3" on page 63) of this tutorial.

> **NOTE**
> If you want to compare your results to the tutorial source file, open the banner1_complete.fla from the FlashBanner/Part1 folder that you saved on your hard disk in "Open the authoring document" on page 163.

Summary

Congratulations for completing your first step of creating a banner in Flash. You used the Flash authoring tool to create a new document, add assets, and manipulate the file using a variety of tools.

In a very short period of time, you learned how to use the Flash workspace to accomplish the following tasks:

- Set up a FLA file.
- Imported assets into the FLA file.
- Arrange assets in a FLA file.
- Create and modify layers.
- Test a SWF file.

You're on your way to creating a banner in Flash so you can embed it in an HTML page using Dreamweaver. In the next two parts of this tutorial, you will create and modify symbols, create an animation, add some simple ActionScript for a button that opens a web page, and add the banner to a website.

To continue building this application, go to the next part of this tutorial: "Basic Tasks: Creating a banner, Part 2" on page 43.

CHAPTER 3

Basic Tasks: Creating a banner, Part 2

3

Welcome to Part 2 of this three-part introduction to Macromedia Flash Basic 8 or Macromedia Flash Professional 8. You successfully completed Part 1 of this tutorial, where you created, set up, and imported content into an FLA file. Because you're reading Part 2, you're probably ready to learn more about Flash. That's good, because you will create symbols, animation, and even write some simple ActionScript to make the banner function in this continuation tutorial. Following this part, you'll add the banner to a website using Dreamweaver (or, you can optionally upload the banner to a website using any tool).

See the introduction to "Basic Tasks: Creating a banner, Part 1" on page 25 for a desecription of Part 1, 2, and 3 of this tutorial.

You do not need any prerequisite knowledge to complete these tutorials, however you should complete Part 1 ("Basic Tasks: Creating a banner, Part 1" on page 25) of this tutorial before you start Part 2.

In Part 2 of this tutorial, you will complete the following tasks:

The tutorial workflow includes the following tasks:

- "Examine the completed FLA file" on page 44 lets you view the completed Flash document for Part 2.

- "Adding text" on page 46 shows you how to create and format text in a FLA file.

- "Creating a symbol" on page 49 shows you how to create a movie clip symbol, to which you'll add an animation.
- "Adding animation to a timeline" on page 51 shows you how to create animation using the main Timeline and motion tweens.
- "Creating a button" on page 56 shows you how to create a button to add interactivity to your banner.
- "Writing simple actions" on page 59 shows you how to write simple ActionScript to make the button work.
- "Test the application" on page 61 shows you how to export and test your document's SWF file, which lets you test your progress so far.

Examine the completed FLA file

As you examine the finished version of an application that you'll create, you'll also look at the Flash workspace.

In this section, you will complete the following tasks:

- "Open the authoring document" on page 163
- "Review the completed FLA file" on page 45
- "Close the completed FLA file" on page 46

In subsequent sections you'll go through the steps to create the application yourself starting with a brand new FLA file.

Open the finished FLA file

The files for this tutorial are located in the Samples and Tutorials folder in the Flash installation folder. For many users, particularly in educational settings, this folder is read-only. Before proceeding with the tutorial, you should copy the entire FlashBanner tutorial folder to the writable location of your choice. In Part 1, you might have already copied the FlashBanner source files to another location of your hard disk.

On most computers, you will find the Flash Banner tutorial folder in the following locations:

- In Windows: *boot drive*\Program Files\Macromedia\Flash 8\ Samples and Tutorials\Tutorial Assets\Basic Tasks\FlashBanner\.
- On the Macintosh: *Macintosh HD*/Applications/Macromedia Flash 8/ Samples and Tutorials/Tutorial Assets/Basic Tasks/FlashBanner/.

Copy the FlashBanner folder to another location on your hard disk to which you have access. Inside this folder are three directories for each part of this tutorial: Part1, Part2, and Part3. In the FlashBanner/Part2 folder, you will find a Flash file called banner2_complete.fla. Double-click the file to open it in Flash. You now see the completed tutorial file in the Flash authoring environment.

Review the completed FLA file

In the completed FLA file, you will see the structure that makes up the finished SWF file for Part 2 of this tutorial. The application, a Flash banner for a gnome website, looks like this at the end of Part 2:

The completed banner for Part 2.

This file contains an animation in a movie clip, text, an invisible button, and the assets that you imported in Part 1 of this tutorial.

- The movie clip instance contains a graphical instance that you animate.
- Text fields contain static, stylized text that you display on the Stage.
- The invisible button covers the entire Stage, and it lets your visitors click the banner and open a new web site.
- The graphic assets include a bitmap background image (the gnome), and the star graphic that you animate in an upcoming exercise.

By the end of Part 3 of this tutorial, you will add the graphics, animation, and interactivity to the banner. Then, you'll insert the banner on a website using Dreamweaver.

Close the completed FLA file

To close the document, select File > Close.

If you prefer to keep the finished file open as a reference while working with your banner file, be careful not to edit it or save any changes to it.

Now you're ready to start creating your own banner file in the next section, "Adding text".

Adding text

You need to add some additional text to your banner for decorative purposes. You can add several types of text to a Flash document: static text, dynamic text, or input text. Static text is useful when you need to add decorative text to the Stage, or any text that doesn't need to change or load from an external source. Use dynamic text when you need to load text from a file, database, or change the text when the SWF file plays in Flash Player. Use input text when you want the user to type into a text field. You can take that text and send it to a database, have it manipulate something in the SWF file, and more.

You can add any of these types of text using the Text tool. For this exercise, you will add some static text to the Stage for decorative purposes. To add static text, follow these steps:

Open the banner.fla file you created in Part 1 of this tutorial, and rename the file **banner2.fla**.

1. Select Insert > Timeline > Layer to insert a new layer. Double-click the layer's name and type **text** to rename the layer.

2. Select the Text tool in the Tools panel, which looks like a large letter A button.

3. Click near the top of the Stage, and type **Overworked?** into the field that's on the Stage.

4. Select the text field (a bounding box appears around the text when you select it).

5. Open the Property inspector (Window > Properties > Properties), and make sure Static Text appears in the Text type pop-up menu.

6. Change the font of the text to whatever font you prefer.

   You change the font using the Font pop-up menu (next to the A icon, seen in the following figure).

7. Select Bitmap text (no anti-alias) in the Font rendering method pop-up menu.

   Anti-alias options help small text appear clearly in your applications, but it makes large text look jagged. Because you're creating large text for the banner, you should use bitmap text which appears smooth when you create large text.

8. Change the size of the font to 20 points using the Font size pop-up menu.

   Then you will need to change the font size so the text fits on the Stage.

Change text settings in the Property inspector.

When you finish, the text should be similar in size and in position to the text in the following figure.

Add some static text to the banner. Select any font you want to use.

9. Select the Text tool again, and type **Underpaid?** below the text you added previously.

10. Select the text field, and open the Property inspector, and then change the text to the same font you selected in the earlier steps.

11. Select a font size so the text is large but still fits on the Stage.

12. Repeat steps 9 through 11 to add the phrase **Gnome?** below the previous two lines of text. When you finish, your banner will resemble the first figure in this tutorial that displays the complete file for Part 2.

13. (Optional) Open the Align panel (Window > Align) to align the text to the center of the Stage. Select a text block on the Stage, click To stage in the Align panel, and then click Align Horizontal center. (Move the mouse over a button in the panel to see what its name is.)

14. Select File > Save to save your progress before moving on.

    After you finish saving the file, proceed to the following exercise, "Creating a symbol".

NOTE | For advanced text effects, you can create text in FreeHand, save the file, and import it. Also, if you're using Adobe Illustrator, you can export the text as a PNG or SWF file. You can then import this text into Flash. You might also investigate FlashType advanced anti-alias options. See "About FlashType" in Flash Help for information.

Creating a symbol

A symbol is an object that you create in Flash. As you discovered in Part 1, a symbol can be a graphic, button, or movie clip, and you can then reuse it throughout the current FLA or other FLA files. Any symbol that you create is automatically added to the document's library (Window > Library), so you can use it many times within a document.

When you add animation, you should always animate symbols in Flash, instead of animating raw graphics (graphics that you draw) or raw assets that you import (such as a PNG file). For example, if you draw a circle using the Oval tool in Flash, you should convert that circle graphic into a movie clip before you animate it. This helps you reduce the SWF file size, and makes it easier to create an animation in Flash.

You will create a movie clip symbol in the following exercise. You will animate this movie clip in later exercises.

1. In banner2.fla, select the star.png image (imported in Part 1) and select Modify > Convert to Symbol from the main menu.

    The Convert to Symbol dialog box opens (see the following figure), where you can name a symbol and select which type of symbol you want it to be.

2. Type **join us** in the Name text box (see the following figure).

    You will see the name of the symbol, join us, in the Library panel after you create the symbol. You will also see an icon that represents movie clips next to the symbol's name.

    Remember that the symbol's name is different than its instance name, because you can have numerous instances of a single symbol on the Stage. For example, you can set an instance name for the join us symbol using the Property inspector after you drag it to the Stage from the Library panel. If you drag another instance of the join us symbol to the Stage, assign it a different instance name. You use the instance name in your ActionScript to reference and manipulate the instance with code. There are some naming guidelines you must follow when you assign an instance name. (This is discussed in "Writing simple actions").

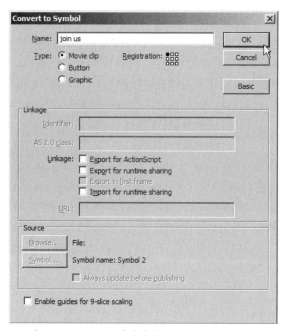

Use the Convert to Symbol dialog box to convert selected content into a symbol, give it a name, and click OK (shown above) add it to the document's library. You might see a smaller dialog box without the advanced linkage and source information when you convert a symbol.

3. Select the Movie clip option, and click OK.

This means that you will convert the graphic image into a movie clip symbol. Movie clip symbols have their own timelines. This means you can animate each movie clip instance on its own timeline, and on the main timeline of the document. This is unique to movie clip instances.

4. Select File > Save to save your progress before moving on.

After you finish saving the file, proceed to the following exercise, "Adding animation to a timeline". In this exercise you will animate the movie clip.

Adding animation to a timeline

You have already used the Timeline in Part 1 of this tutorial ("Basic Tasks: Creating a banner, Part 1" on page 25) to insert new layers and add content onto those layers. In Part 1 you added assets to a frame on the Timeline. You might have noticed that after you add content on a frame, a filled circle appears on the frame to signify content on that frame. Whenever there's new or changed content on a frame, it's called a keyframe and has a filled black dot on the frame. A keyframe is a frame where you define changes in the animation, or a frame that has content on it. An empty keyframe has a hollow circle.

You create an animation in a Flash document by adding content to a timeline, such as the main timeline, or a timeline inside a movie clip. When the playhead moves across the Timeline, those individual frames play and when played in quick succession (like a flipbook or succession of frames on a reel of film), you can create an animation.

When you create a frame-by-frame animation, every frame is a keyframe. In a tweened animation, you define keyframes at significant points in the animation and let Flash create the contents of frames in between. Flash displays the interpolated frames of a tweened animation as light blue or light green with an arrow drawn between keyframes. Because Flash documents save the shapes in each keyframe, you should create keyframes only at the points in the animation where something changes.

1. Select Modify > Document.

    The Document Properties dialog box opens. This is the dialog box you used to change the dimensions of the banner in Part 1 of this tutorial. Now you want to change the frame rate for the banner.

2. Change the number in the frame rate text box to **18**, and then click OK to apply the new setting.

    A higher frame rate means that your animation plays smoothly, more so than when you had it set to 12 frames per second (fps). Changing the fps setting means that the main timeline and movie clip timelines all play at the specified frame rate.

> **NOTE**
>
> An increased frame rate also means that there is a slightly increased demand on the user's computer (or CPU) to render the extra frames each second.

3. Double-click the join us symbol instance on the Stage.

This opens the symbol in symbol-editing mode (see the following figure). In this mode, you see the movie clip symbol's timeline, which runs independently of the timeline for the main FLA file (the one you saw before double-clicking the symbol). This means you can have animations that play and stop independently from animations on the main timeline. Remember that a movie clip still plays at the document's frame rate (18 fps).

In symbol-editing mode, the symbol that you're editing appears normal, while other items on the Stage are dimmed. Changes that you make in this mode apply to every instance of the symbol in your FLA file. Notice how the edit bar (above the Timeline in this figure) changes to show you what you're editing, and its relation to the main Stage.

When you enter this mode, it means you edit the symbol itself, not just the single instance on the Stage. Any changes you make on this timeline (which is the movie clip's timeline) apply to every instance of the symbol that you use in the FLA file.

You can tell that you're editing a symbol by looking at the edit bar (see the top of the previous image). Use the edit bar to navigate throughout a document. The edit bar might be above or below the Timeline, depending on how you have the workspace set up.

Scene 1 refers to the main timeline of the FLA file. You can click this button on the edit bar to return to the main timeline. The names after it point to the symbol that you're editing. If the symbol is nested within other symbols, this path might contain several names. In the previous figure, you can see that you're editing the join us symbol that's on the main timeline (Scene 1).

4. Select the PNG file that's inside the movie clip, and then press F8 to convert it into another symbol.

5. In the Convert to Symbol dialog box, type the name **nested mc** in the Name text box, select Movie clip, and click OK.

6. Select Frame 15 and select Insert > Timeline > Keyframe.

> **NOTE**
> Press F6 to quickly insert a new keyframe.

This command inserts a new keyframe, which means you can modify the content on that frame to create animation. Currently, the content on Frame 15 is duplicated from the content on Frame 1. When you modify Frame 15 in a future step, the modifications won't change the content on Frame 1.

7. Select Frame 30 and press F6 to insert a new keyframe.

The keyframe duplicates the content from Frame 15. That means the content on all three frames is the same.

8. Select the movie clip instance on Frame 15, and open the Property inspector (Window > Properties > Properties).

> **NOTE**
> Make sure you select the instance on Frame 15, not just the frame. You can first select the frame on the Timeline (or move the playhead to Frame 15), and then select the movie clip instance on the Stage in order to see the correct context of the Property inspector, as shown in the following figure.

9. Select Brightness from the Color pop-up menu (the following figure).

10. Change the slider value to 75% (see the following figure).

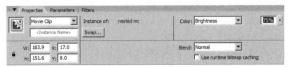

Change the brightness of the movie clip instance.

The brightness changes for the instance on Frame 15. The instances on Frames 1 and 30 do not change. This means that you can now add a motion tween that animates the brightness value between Frames 1 and 15, and then from Frames 15 to 30. After playing Frame 30, the playhead loops back to Frame 1 and the animation starts again.

> **NOTE**
> You could also change the alpha or tint values using the same procedure. Alpha tweens are more processor intensive than tweens that change the brightness or tint of your animation. Try to avoid processor-intensive procedures whenever possible.

11. Select the instance on the Stage at Frame 15 again, and then select the Free Transform tool in the Tools panel. Select the lower right handle and drag it towards the center of the image to make it smaller (see the following figure).

Resize the instance using the Free Transform tool. As shown in this figure, you can also rotate the image using the Free Transform tool.

You can create several kinds of animation in an FLA file, such as motion tweens, shape tweens, and frame-by-frame animation. In this tutorial, you will create a motion tween. A motion tween is an animation where you define properties such as position, size, and rotation for an instance at one point in time, and then you change those properties at another point in time. In this animation, you change the brightness and size of the instance.

12. Select any frame between Frames 1 and 15, and then select Motion from the Tween pop-up menu in the Property inspector.

   The span of frames changes color and an arrow appears between Frames 1 and 15 (see the following figure). Notice how the options in the Property inspector are different when you select a frame compared to when you select a movie clip instance.

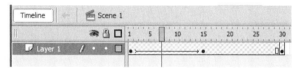

Create a motion tween between Frames 1 and 15 on the movie clip's timeline.

NOTE | You can also right-click (Windows) or option-click (Macintosh) the frame and select Create Motion Tween from the context menu instead.

13. Select any frame between Frames 15 and 30, and then select Motion from the Tween pop-up menu in the Property inspector to create a second animation.

14. Click the playhead and drag it across the movie clip's timeline to test (or scrub) the animation.

15. Select Control > Test Movie.

> **NOTE** A quicker way to test your SWF file is to use keyboard shortcuts. Press Control + Enter (Windows) or Command + Return (Macintosh) to test the file.

The test environment opens where you can see the animation. Notice how it loops, appearing to fade in and out because of the change in brightness. By default, the playhead returns to Frame 1 and replays the animation after it reaches the final frame on the Timeline. This means the animation loops repeatedly, unless you tell it to stop. You will find out how to do this below in the exercise called "Writing simple actions".

16. Select File > Save to save your progress before moving on.

After you finish saving the file, proceed to the following exercise, "Creating a button".

Creating a button

When you create a banner, you need to let your user click anywhere in the banner area and open a new browser window. You can create buttons very easily in Flash. Your button can either have a graphic with rollover graphics, sounds, and even animations of their own. Or, you can create an invisible button. Invisible buttons are useful when you want to create "hot spots" on your website, or make the entire banner clickable without obscuring your graphics. In the following exercise, you'll add an invisible button over your banner graphics.

> **NOTE** For more information on creating visible buttons with graphics and rollover effects, search creating buttons in the Flash Help panel (F1).

1. Click Scene 1 in the edit bar to make sure that you're on the main Stage.

2. Select Insert > Timeline > Layer to create a new layer, and rename the new layer to **button**.

3. Select the Rectangle tool in the Tools panel (the button's icon looks like a square).

4. Find the Colors section of the Tools panel (see the following figure), and click the pencil icon to select the Stroke color control.

5. Select No Color, as shown in the following figure. Doing so disables the rectangle's outline.

Select No Color for the stroke color control.

6. Drag the mouse diagonally across the Stage to create a rectangle.

The size of the rectangle does not matter—you'll resize it later using the Property inspector.

7. Click the Selection tool in the Tools panel, and click the rectangle on the Stage to select it.

A cross-hatch pattern appears over the rectangle when you select it.

8. Open the Property inspector (Window > Properties > Properties).

9. Change the value in the W (width) text box to **160** and the H (height) text box to **600**. Then change the X text box and the Y text box both to **0** (see the following figure).

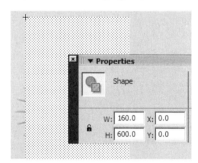

Change the width and height of the rectangle, and then set the location of the rectangle to cover the Stage.

10. With the rectangle still selected on the Stage, press F8 to change the rectangle into a symbol.

11. In the Convert to Symbol dialog box, type **inv btn** in the Name text box, select Button, and then click OK.

12. Double-click the new button on the Stage to enter the Symbol-editing mode.

The rectangle is currently on the first Up frame of the button you created. This is the Up state of the button—what users see when the button sits on the Stage. Instead, you want the button not to have anything visible on the Stage. Therefore, you need to move the rectangle to the Hit frame, which is the hit area of the button (the active region that a user can click to activate the button's actions).

13. Click the keyframe at the Up frame, and hold down the mouse button while you drag the keyframe to the Hit frame (see the following figure).

Drag the rectangle keyframe from the Up frame to the Hit frame on the Timeline.

Now the entire area of the banner is clickable, but there is no visual appearance of the button on your banner.

14. Click Scene 1 to return to the main Timeline.

Now there is a teal rectangle over the banner area. This refers to the invisible button's Hit area. If it's distracting to you, you can hide the button layer in the authoring environment.

15. (Optional) On the Timeline, click the dot that's under the Eye icon on the button layer to hide the contents of that layer.

16. Select File > Save to save your progress before moving on.

After you finish saving the file, proceed to the following exercise, "Writing simple actions".

Writing simple actions

You need to add some simple ActionScript to your banner in order for the invisible button to open a website or send information about how many clicks the banner has received.

There are several different places you can add ActionScript in a Flash document. You can select an instance, and add ActionScript that attaches directly to that instance. To access the code, you would need to find and select that instance again. You can also add ActionScript to a frame (or multiple frames) on the Timeline. It's a good idea to add all of your code to a single frame on the Timeline, because it's much easier to find, update, and organize when you're working on a file. Do not attach your ActionScript to instances.

NOTE
You can also keep your ActionScript in external class files that import into the FLA file you're working on. This is sometimes the best way to organize your ActionScript, particularly when you work on larger projects. This topic goes beyond the scope of this tutorial.

Notice how your Join Us motion tween continually loops when you test it. By default, the playhead on the Timeline loops if you have content on more than one frame. Therefore, if you have content on several frames in a movie clip or on the main Timeline, it will play and loop forever. You can stop the playhead from looping by adding a single line of ActionScript. If you add this ActionScript to a frame, the playhead stops when it reaches that frame:

```
stop();
```

You don't need to add this ActionScript to your banner. However, you will need to add this ActionScript to other FLA files that you create. The stop action is ActionScript you need to know about when you start using Flash so you can stop looping SWF files when necessary.

Before you add the code, you need to give the button a unique instance name. The instance name enables you to target the button with ActionScript code. If you don't name the button, your code doesn't have a way of targeting the button from the timeline. The first step is to assign the invisible button an instance name, and then you add code that targets that button using its name.

1. Select the invisible button on the Stage.

2. Open the Property inspector (Window > Properties), and find the Instance Name text box in the Property inspector.

3. Type **inv_btn** into the Instance Name text box.

> **NOTE** An instance name is different from the symbols name (which is what you type in the Name text box in the Convert to Symbol dialog box). An instance name cannot have spaces or special characters, but you can use underscores. Also, your instance names are case-sensitive.

4. Select Insert > Timeline > Layer to insert a new layer, and then rename the new layer to **actions**.

5. Open the Actions panel (Window > Actions), and then select Frame 1 of the actions layer.

6. Type the following ActionScript into the script pane (the editable text field) in the Actions panel:

```
inv_btn.onRelease = function(){
    getURL("http://gnome.deseloper.com", "_blank");
};
```

Notice how you target the `inv_btn` instance in the first line of code. The event is the `onRelease` event in your ActionScript code, which refers to the action when a user clicks and then releases the mouse over the `inv_btn` instance. Then you tell the button to open a particular web page (http://gnome.deseloper.com) in a new window (_blank) using the `getURL()` method. Obviously, you would replace this URL with whatever website you want the banner to open. If you want the banner to open the website in the current page, replace _blank with _self.

This is a simple piece of ActionScript code that reacts to a button click. There is a lot of additional information on learning the ActionScript language in the Flash 8 help. In Flash, choose Help > Flash Help and find *Learning ActionScript 2.0 in Flash* in the Table of Contents.

7. Select File > Save to save your progress before moving on.

After you finish saving the file, proceed to the following exercise, "Test the application".

Test the application

Now you have a Flash banner, with graphics and animation, which also reacts to button clicks. You have completed your first interactive and animated Flash document. Let's take a look at it in action, within a browser window.

1. Return to your banner2 document, and then select File > Publish Preview > HTML.

The default browser on your computer opens and displays the banner. By default, the banner appears at the upper-left corner of the HTML document.

2. Click the banner to open the web page. A new browser window should open and display the gnome website.

3. Close both browser windows and return to the Flash authoring environment.

If you are happy with your document, then save your changes and stay posted for Part 3 of this tutorial. You might want to change the animation or text, or modify the code as necessary.

> **NOTE** If you want to compare your results to the tutorial source file, open the banner2_complete.fla from the FlashBanner/Part2 folder that you saved on your hard disk in "Open the authoring document" on page 163.

Summary

Congratulations for completing the next step of creating a banner in Flash. You used the Flash authoring tool to add text, create symbols, animate on a timeline, and add interactivity to your application. In Part 2 of this tutorial, you learned how to use the Flash workspace to accomplish the following tasks:

- Create text.
- Create symbols.
- Create an animation.
- Create buttons.
- Write ActionScript.

You now have a banner that you can export and add to a web page. In Part 3 of this tutorial, you will publish your work, and take the file and add it to a Dreamweaver website.

To continue building this application, go to the Part 3 of this tutorial: "Basic Tasks: Creating a banner, Part 3" on page 63.

CHAPTER 4

Basic Tasks: Creating a banner, Part 3

4

This is Part 3 of a three-part article on how to build a simple animated banner in Macromedia Flash Basic 8 or Macromedia Flash Professional 8, and add it to a web page using Macromedia Dreamweaver. In this final part, you learn about file size, banner standards, how to set publish settings, how to add the banner to a Dreamweaver web page, and how to add Macromedia Flash Player detection.

You must have Dreamweaver MX 2004 or Dreamweaver 8 installed to complete most of Part 3 of the tutorial. If you don't use Dreamweaver, you can complete the first part of this article and use the HTML that Flash outputs with a different HTML editor. However, you won't be able to enjoy some of the benefits of using Flash and Dreamweaver together.

See the introduction to "Basic Tasks: Creating a banner, Part 1" on page 25 for a desecription of Part 1, 2, and 3 of this tutorial.

You do not need any prerequisite knowledge to complete these tutorials, however you should complete Part 1 and Part 2 of this tutorial before you start Part 3.

In Part 3 of this tutorial, you will complete the following tasks:

The tutorial workflow includes the following tasks:

- "Examine the completed FLA file" on page 65 lets you view the completed Flash document for Part 3.

- "Checking your publish settings" on page 68 shows you how to check and modify your publish settings before you compile the finished banner.

- "Inserting Flash on a Dreamweaver site" on page 71 shows you how to insert a Flash animation into a web page using Dreamweaver.

- "Using roundtrip editing" on page 73 shows you how to return to the Flash authoring tool from Dreamweaver to make further modifications of your FLA file.

- "Checking for Flash Player" on page 74 shows you how to add a Dreamweaver behavior that detects if your visitor has Flash Player installed.

- "Test the application" on page 76 shows you how to export and test your document's SWF file, which lets you test your progress so far.

Examine the completed FLA file

As you examine the finished version of an application that you'll create, you'll also look at the Flash workspace.

In this section, you will complete the following tasks:

- "Open the authoring document" on page 163
- "Review the completed FLA file" on page 164
- "Close the completed project" on page 66

In subsequent sections you'll go through the steps to create the application yourself starting with a brand new FLA file.

Open the finished project

The files for this tutorial are located in the Samples and Tutorials folder in the Flash installation folder. For many users, particularly in educational settings, this folder is read-only. Before proceeding with the tutorial, you should copy the entire FlashBanner tutorial folder to the writable location of your choice. In Part 1 or Part 2, you might have already copied the FlashBanner source files to another location of your hard disk.

On most computers, you will find the Flash Banner tutorial folder in the following locations:

- In Windows: *boot drive*\Program Files\Macromedia\Flash 8\ Samples and Tutorials\Tutorial Assets\Basic Tasks\FlashBanner\.
- On the Macintosh: *Macintosh HD*/Applications/Macromedia Flash 8/ Samples and Tutorials/Tutorial Assets/Basic Tasks/FlashBanner/.

Copy the FlashBanner folder to another location on your hard disk to which you have access. Inside this folder are three directories for each part of this tutorial: Part1, Part2, and Part3. In the FlashBanner/Part3 folder, you will find an HTML file called gnome.html inside the finished folder. Double-click the file to open it in your default browser. You now see the completed SWF and HTML files in the browser window.

Review the completed project

In the completed project, you will see the structure that makes up the finished project for Part 3 of this tutorial. The application, a Flash banner inserted into an HTML page for a gnome website, looks like this at the end of Part 3:

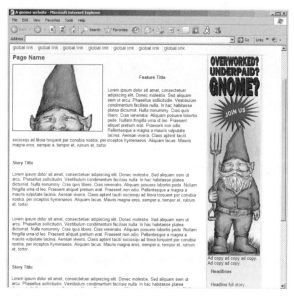

The completed banner for Part 3

By the end of Part 3 of this tutorial, you will add the banner that you created which contains graphics, animation, and interactivity to a website using Dreamweaver.

Close the completed project

To close the document, click the close button on your browser window, in the upper right (Windows) or left (Macintosh) corner of the window.

You might prefer to keep the finished file open as a reference while working with your banner file.

Now you're ready to start creating your own banner file in the next section, "Considering your audience".

Considering your audience

When you create a site, you often need to follow certain guidelines for submitting a Flash banner. For the purposes of this article, following established advertising guidelines is not a great concern because you're not submitting the banner to a company for advertising purposes. This section briefly explores some of the considerations you might have when creating a banner in a real-life project, or a project for wide distribution. When you create a banner that you submit to an advertising company, often you need to make sure the file meets their specified file size, dimension, target Flash Player version, and frame-rate guidelines. Sometimes, you have to consider other rules about the kinds of media you can use, button code you use in the FLA file, and so forth.

You have created the banner and resized its dimensions. When doing so, you actually set the banner to established and standardized dimensions for what the Interactive Advertising Bureau calls a "wide skyscraper." The file size is also reasonable for a Flash ad of this size. You will discover how to reduce the file size in an upcoming exercise. For information on standard advertising dimensions (and many other useful guidelines), check out the Interactive Advertising Bureau's Standards and Guidelines page here: www.iab.net/standards/adunits.asp. However, ensure you confirm the advertising guidelines for the advertising service, client, or website that you're advertising with first. Guidelines might include standards for file size, dimensions, sound and video usage, and buttons.

The purpose of this article is understand how to create Flash content, export it from Flash, and add it to your own website. The lesson to draw from considering banner guidelines is that you need to consider your audience. Whenever you create a Flash site, think about the kind of people who will see the content—much like when you create any website. Is your audience a wide range of individuals, with many kinds of computers and Flash Players (or none at all)? Or, is your audience primarily fellow Flash developers and new media companies? Your audience affects which Flash Player version you target. For example, if you think a diverse audience (often a large audience with a wide range of computer capabilities) will visit your site, target an earlier version of Flash Player, such as version 6. If you think other web professionals will visit the site, then the latest player (with a detection system) is fine. You set your Flash Player and add a Flash Player detection system using Dreamweaver in upcoming sections.

> **NOTE**
> If you send your banner to a company to host, they usually have special requirements for how you add button code to your FLA file. Often, they want you to add a specific variable (such as clickTAG) instead of a URL. Refer to the advertising service, client, or website guidelines for the correct button code to add to your FLA file. Some companies also limit what frames per second (fps) rate you can use in the SWF file. When you design a banner, try to keep your fps rate as low as possible. I recommend using 18 fps or lower; ideally, use 12 fps.

Checking your publish settings

Often you need to save banners to earlier versions of Flash Player. Many sites you might advertise with now accept Flash Player 6 files. You might also create a website that targets a wide audience, and you need to target an older player. The simple ActionScript you added to your file can play in Flash Player 6. Therefore, you can change your player settings to Flash Player 6 for your website.

In earlier parts of this tutorial, you made changes in the Document Settings dialog box. You set the dimensions and frame rate (fps) for the SWF file. In this final section, you will make sure that the Flash Player setting you want to target is correct, and that you export the files you need. Many Flash developers make these settings when they start the FLA file, because they are aware of what they need to output and target.

1. Open the banner2.fla file from Part 2 of this tutorial ("Basic Tasks: Creating a banner, Part 2").

    If you don't have banner2.fla, open banner3.fla from the tutorial source files (see "Open the finished project" on page 65). Look inside the start folder.

2. Select File > Save As and then rename the file **banner3.fla**.

3. Select File > Publish Settings.

    The Publish Setting dialog box opens, where you can change many different settings for publishing your files.

4. Click the Formats tab, and then make sure that the Flash (.swf) check box is selected.

5. Deselect the HTML option.

    For this exercise, you don't need to output an HTML page.

6. Click the Flash tab, and select Flash Player 6 from the Version pop-up menu.

    When you add Flash advertisements to an HTML page, use Flash Player 6 or earlier (as of the time of writing). Many Flash developers still use Flash Player 5, although sites are starting to use Flash Player 6, which enables you to add additional functionality in your Flash advertisements.

7. Select ActionScript 1.0 from the ActionScript version pop-up menu.

    For this example, you wrote ActionScript 1.0 style code (in Part 2), and although this setting does not matter it's a good habit to check which version you have selected. You can write ActionScript 2.0 and publish to Flash Player 6 if you want.

8. In the Options section, select Compress movie.

   You do not need to make any other selections on the Flash tab.

9. When you finish, click OK to accept the changes to your document.

10. Select File > Publish when you have finished editing your FLA file.

    This publishes the SWF file to the directory where you saved the SWF file.

11. Go to the directory to which you published the banner's SWF file. Check the file size of the document (it's called banner3.swf).

    As discussed previously, file size is not a great concern because you're not submitting the banner to an advertising service. If you need to or want to reduce the file size of your banner, you can go to the Publish Settings dialog box again (File > Publish Settings) and click the Flash tab. You can reduce the quality of the bitmap image you use in the background by changing the JPEG quality to a lower number.

12. Move the slider to 60, and click Publish.

    When you check the SWF file again, the file size is smaller.

There are other ways to reduce the file size of a SWF file. If you need to design a file to a specific maximum file size, make sure you publish your work regularly and check the current file size. Bitmap images, sounds, and video quickly increase a SWF file's size.

If you don't have Dreamweaver installed, then the tutorial series ends with this section. If you don't have Dreamweaver, you can return to the Publish Settings dialog box from this exercise, and make sure you select the HTML option under the Formats tab. When you publish the document, an HTML file exports with the SWF file. You can open this file, copy the HTML code, and paste it into your website. Notice that this file contains some extra tags that you won't need if you have an existing website, such as head and body tags. The tags you need are both the object and embed tags, which contains the information both Internet Explorer and Mozilla-based browsers need to display the SWF file.

If you have Dreamweaver installed, continue to the next page. In the following exercises, you place and edit the banner in a web page.

Inserting Flash on a Dreamweaver site

You might have a web page already created for a banner. We have created a page for you to use for the purposes of this exercise, which is ready to have a banner of this size placed on it.

Make sure that you have the FlashBanner/Part3 directory available (see "Open the finished project"), and find the website folder inside this directory. Inside the website folder are the documents that you need to edit in Dreamweaver. You will modify the gnome.html web page in the following exercise.

> **NOTE**
> You can find a finished version of the website in the finished folder in the FlashBanner/Part3 directory.

1. Open the page called gnome.html in Dreamweaver MX 2004 or Dreamweaver 8 (this tutorial uses Dreamweaver 8).

    You can find this document in the website folder of this article's source files. Look inside the start folder (FlashBanner/Part3/website/start).

2. Save a copy of gnome.html in the same directory as the SWF file you published in the previous exercise (banner3.swf).

3. Save a copy of rightnav.css in the same directory as the SWF file you published in the previous exercise.

    Look inside the start folder to find rightnav.css. This document adds styles (such as text color and margins) to the gnome.html file.

4. In Dreamweaver, make sure that you're in Split view (View > Code and Design).

    When in Split view, you can see and edit the code you're working on, and also select the SWF file easily in Design view.

5. Select the large 160 x 600 image placeholder on the right side of the web page (see the following figure).

This is where you want to add the Flash banner to the website.

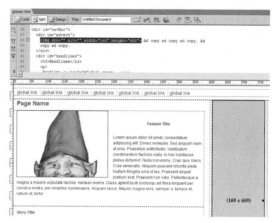

Select the large image placeholder on the right side of the web page in Dreamweaver. Notice that the dimensions are the same as your banner file.

6. Press the Backspace or Delete key to delete the image. Leave the text selection pointer at that position in the HTML document.

7. Select Insert > Media > Flash.

This opens the Select File dialog box, where you can select the SWF file of the banner you created.

8. Select the banner3.swf file, which should be in the same folder your web page is in (see Step 2).

9. Click OK.

The SWF file is inserted into the web page. (See the gnome.html document in the finished folder to reference the code that's added to the document).

10. (Optional) You can select the SWF file and click Play in the Property inspector to view the banner's animation.

11. Select File > Preview in Browser > iexplore (Windows) or Internet Explorer (Macintosh) (or select your preferred browser) to preview your site that now contains the SWF banner in a browser window.

12. Select File > Save in Dreamweaver to save your changes before you proceed to "Using roundtrip editing".

Using roundtrip editing

By now, you might want to change something in your Flash banner. Say you want to change the frame rate, or add some more text. It's easy to return to Flash to edit the document from Dreamweaver.

1. In gnome.html, select the SWF file in Design view (where you see the layout of the page below the HTML code), and then open the Property inspector (Window > Properties).

    The Property inspector displays controls for the SWF file.

2. Click Edit in the Property inspector (see the following figure).

    Select the SWF file and click Edit in the Property inspector.

    Flash opens the associated FLA file in the Flash authoring environment, or opens a window for you to locate the associated FLA file.

3. Make your edits in Flash.

    Notice that "Editing From Dreamweaver" displays in the authoring environment, to indicate you're editing a file from the Dreamweaver environment.

4. Click Done next to Editing From Dreamweaver (see the following figure).

    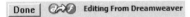

    You can edit the FLA file directly from Dreamweaver. Click Done when you're finished.

    Flash updates the FLA file, publishes the SWF file, closes Flash, and then returns you to the Dreamweaver document. Your document is updated in Dreamweaver.

> **NOTE** To view the changes to your SWF file in Dreamweaver, either view your site in a browser or select the SWF file in Design view and click Play in the Property inspector.

Checking for Flash Player

Most people who visit your website will have the Flash Player 6 or greater plug-in installed. In rare circumstances, a visitor might not have the plug-in installed. There are several different things you can do when a visitor without Flash Player visits your site. When you have a site that uses Flash primarily for functionality, you might want to send that user to a custom page that links to the Macromedia site, where the user can download the player.

The Check Plugin behavior in Dreamweaver enables you to check whether visitors to your website have the Flash Player plug-in installed. After the behavior checks for a plug-in, you can route the visitor to different URLs, depending on whether they have the minimum required plug-in. For example, if the visitor doesn't have Flash Player, you can open a page that links the visitor to the Macromedia website to download the latest version.

1. In gnome.html, click inside the body tag (click between the "y" the closing angle bracket) and open the Behaviors panel in Dreamweaver (Window > Behaviors).

2. Click Add (+) and select Check Plugin from the behaviors pop-up menu.

3. Select Flash from the Plugin pop-up menu.

4. Leave the If Found, Go To URL text box blank.

   This text box controls which page the visitor with the specified plug-in sees. Leaving the text box blank ensures that users stays on the same page if they have Flash Player installed.

5. Type a URL into the Otherwise, Go To URL text box.

   Specify an alternative URL for visitors who don't have the Flash Player plug-in. Type noflash.html into the text box.

> **NOTE** There is a noflash.html document for you with the source files, included in the sample files that accompany this tutorial; it's inside the finished folder. Either save this document in the same folder as the gnome.html document you're working on, or create your own file in this location. Ideally, you would create a custom web page for users without Flash Player.

6. Select the Always go to first URL if detection is not possible option.

   When selected, this option effectively means "assume that the visitor has the plug-in, unless the browser explicitly indicates that the plug-in is not present." Because you add an alternate ad for visitors without the plug-in, this option is preferable for this exercise. The following figure shows the selections you have made up to this point to add Flash Player detection.

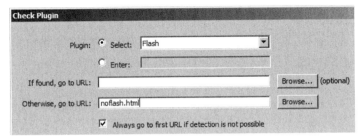

Make these selections to add Flash Player detection in Dreamweaver using a behavior.

7. Click OK. When you finish, Dreamweaver adds the following code to the <body> tag:

```
<body id="container" onLoad="MM_checkPlugin('Shockwave
   Flash','','noflash.html',true);return
   document.MM_returnValue">
```

8. Save your changes to the document before you proceed to "Test the application".

> **NOTE**
>
> You can find the finished files in the FlashBanner/Part3 file directory, inside the finished folder.

You can also add Flash Player detection in Flash authoring if you aren't using Dreamweaver. Go to the Publish Settings dialog box (File > Publish Settings) and make sure that you select HTML in the Formats tab. Then select the HTML tab, and select the Detect Flash Version option. Click Settings next to the check box. You can set the target, content, and alternate pages in this dialog box.

Test the application

Now you have a Flash banner, with graphics and animation, which also reacts to button clicks. You have completed your first interactive and animated Flash document, and then you inserted it into a website using Dreamweaver. Let's take a look at the banner in action, within a browser window.

1. Click the gnome.html document that you modified in the previous exercises to open the web page that contains your banner.

    A new browser window opens and display the gnome website.

2. Click the banner to open the browser window from the web page.

> **NOTE** If you want to compare your results to the tutorial source file, open the banner3_complete.fla and gnome.html files from the finished folder inside the FlashBanner/Part3 folder that you saved on your hard disk in "Open the authoring document" on page 163.

Summary

Now you have completed your first Flash site and inserted it into a Dreamweaver web page. You have learned how to create a new file, import content, create new assets in Flash, add simple animation and ActionScript, and publish your work for the web. You also learned how to use Dreamweaver to insert the SWF file into an existing web page, probably one that's similar to a simple page you've created in the past.

In Part 3 of this tutorial, you learned how to use Flash and Dreamweaver to accomplish the following tasks:

- Modify publish settings for a SWF file.
- Publish a SWF file.
- Insert a SWF file on a web page using Dreamweaver.
- Use roundtrip editing to open, modify, and republish a FLA file from Dreamweaver.
- Add a Dreamweaver behavior to check for Flash Player.

This introductory step of learning Flash and adding a SWF file to a web page is an important one when you're learning to use Flash. You now have the fundamentals and understand the essential nature and workflow of creating content with Flash. Hopefully, you'll feel better equipped to learn how to create increasingly interactive, entertaining, functional, or instructional content using Flash.

CHAPTER 5

Basic Tasks: Create Accessible Flash Content

5

With knowledge of a few design techniques and accessibility features in Macromedia Flash Basic 8 and Macromedia Flash Professional 8, you can create Flash content that is accessible to all users, including those with disabilities.

This lesson demonstrates how to create an accessible document, designed for use with screen readers (which read web content aloud for visually impaired users) and other assistive technologies.

You can print this tutorial by downloading a PDF version of it from the Macromedia Flash Documentation page at www.macromedia.com/go/fl_documentation.

In this tutorial, you will complete the following tasks:

The lesson offers an introduction to basic techniques of making your Flash content accessible. For detailed and comprehensive information about incorporating accessibility features in your Flash content, see "Creating Accessible Content" in Flash Help.

Set up your workspace

First, you'll open the start file for the lesson and set up your workspace to use an optimal layout for taking lessons.

1. To open your start file, in Flash select File > Open and navigate to the file:

    -   In Windows, browse to *boot drive*\Program Files\Macromedia\ Flash 8\Samples and Tutorials\Tutorial Assets\Basic Tasks\ Create Accessible Content and double-click accessibility_start.fla.

    -   On the Macintosh, browse to *Macintosh HD*/Applications/ Macromedia Flash 8/Samples and Tutorials/Tutorial Assets/ Basic Tasks/Create Accessible Content and double-click accessibility_start.fla.

2. Select File > Save As and save the document with a new name, in the same folder, to preserve the original start file.

> As you complete this lesson, remember to save your work frequently.

3. Select Window > Workspace Layout > Default to set up your workspace for taking lessons.

Make your document accessible to screen readers

You'll now specify that your document is accessible to screen readers, and provide a name and description of your document that a screen reader can read aloud.

1. With nothing selected on the Stage, select Window > Other Panels > Accessibility.

2. In the Accessibility panel, verify that the following options are selected:

   Make Movie Accessible is selected by default and allows Flash Player to pass accessibility information to a screen reader.

   Make Child Objects Accessible allows Flash Player to pass accessibility information nested inside a movie clip to a screen reader. If this option is selected for the entire document, you can still hide child objects for individual movie clips.

   Auto Label associates text next to another Stage object, such as an input text field, as a label or title for that element.

Provide a document title and description

In the Accessibility panel for the document, you can enter a name and description for your document for screen readers.

- In the Name text box, enter **Trio ZX2004**. In the Description text box, enter **Corporate website about the Trio ZX2004. Includes 6 navigation buttons, overview text, and an animated car.**

Provide a title and description for instances

Now that you've provided information about the entire document, you can provide information about Stage objects included in the document.

1. Select the Trio Motor Company logo along the top of the Stage. In the Accessibility panel, enter **Trio Motor Company** in the Name text box. Do not enter anything in the Description text box.

    Not every instance needs a description, which is read with the title information. If the title name sufficiently describes the function of the object, you don't need to include a description.

2. With the Accessibility panel still open, select the Dealers button on the Stage.

    Information in the Accessibility panel changes to reflect Accessibility options for the selected object.

    In the Accessibility panel for the Dealers button, you do not need to provide a name in the Title text box, because the button includes a text label that the screen reader will read. If you did not want the screen reader to read the text in the button, you could deselect Auto Label when you set up accessibility for the document.

3. In the Description text box, enter **Links to a web page with information about dealers nationwide**.

The other buttons also include text, which the screen reader will read aloud; therefore, you do not need to provide a title. Since the title of the buttons is fairly self-explanatory, there's no need for you to include descriptions.

Specify that screen readers ignore elements in your document

Screen readers follow a specific order when reading web content. However, when content on the web page changes, most screen readers will begin reading the web content all over again. This screen reader feature can be problematic when Flash content contains, for example, animation, which could cause the screen reader to begin again each time there's a change in the animation.

Fortunately, you can use the Accessibility panel to either deselect Make Object Accessible, so that the screen reader does not receive accessibility information about the object, or deselect Make Child Objects Accessible, so that the screen reader does not receive accessibility information nested within a movie clip. You'll now do the latter so that users will know the web page contains an animation, and the animation won't cause the screen reader to constantly refresh.

1. On the Stage, click the car, which is the safety_mc movie clip instance.

2. In the Accessibility panel, deselect Make Child Objects Accessible. In the Name text box, enter **Trio ZX2004 animation**. In the Description text box, enter **Animation that includes three views of the Trio ZX2004**.

Change static text to dynamic text for accessibility

Static text is accessible to screen readers. However, you cannot provide static text with an instance name, which is required to control the tab order and reading order. You'll change the overview text paragraph to dynamic text and specify accessibility options.

1. On the Stage, select the text that begins "The TRIO ZX2004 provides the ultimate in efficiency...."

   The Accessibility panel changes to indicate that you cannot apply accessibility features to this selection.

2. In the Property inspector, select Dynamic Text from the Text Type pop-up menu.

   Accessibility settings now appear in the Accessibility panel.

3. In the Instance name text box, enter **text9_txt**.

To specify a tab order and reading order, which you'll do next, you must provide an instance name for all instances. The instance name must be unique in your document.

Control the tab order and reading order

You can create a tab order that determines the order in which objects receive focus when the users press the Tab key. You can also control the order in which a screen reader reads information about the object (known as the reading order). You can create both the tab and reading order using the `tabIndex` property in ActionScript (In ActionScript, the `tabIndex` property is synonymous with the reading order). If you have Flash Professional 8, you can use the Accessibility panel to specify the tab order, but the tab index that you assign does not necessarily control the reading order.

To create a reading order, you must assign a tab index to every instance in ActionScript.

If you have Flash Professional, creating a tab order is as easy as entering a number in the Tab Index text box. You can then view the tab order directly on the Stage.

To create a tab order in this lesson, use one of the following procedures. To create a reading order along with a tab order, follow the procedure to control the tab order and reading order using ActionScript.

If you have Flash Professional 8, you can follow this procedure to create a tab order using the Accessibility panel:

1. With the Accessibility panel open, select the logo_mc instance at the top of the Stage. In the Accessibility panel, enter **1** in the Tab Index text box.

2. Continue to select each instance on the Stage and enter a tab order number in the Tab Index text box, using information from the following table:

Instance name	Enter the following number in the Tab Index text box
logo_mc	1
dealers_btn	2
orders_btn	3
research_btn	4
text4_txt (the text above the Overview button that reads TRIO ZX2004)	5
overview_btn	6
powerplant_btn	7
news_btn	8
safety_mc	9
text8_txt	10
text9_txt	11
bevel_mc (the bar along the bottom of the Stage)	12

If you have Flash Professional 8, follow this procedure to view a tab order:

■ Select View > Show Tab Order.

The tab index number that you entered appears next to the instance on the Stage.

Follow this procedure to control the tab order and reading order using ActionScript:

1. In the Timeline, select Frame 1 of the Actions layer.

2. In the Actions panel (Window > Actions), view the ActionScript that creates the tab index for each instance in the document.

3. If you're using Flash Basic 8, or if you're using Flash Professional 8 and you did not create the tab index using the Accessibility panel, delete the /* and */ in the script to uncomment the script:

```
this.logo_mc.tabIndex = 1;
this.dealers_btn.tabIndex = 2;
this.orders_btn.tabIndex = 3;
this.research_btn.tabIndex = 4;
this.text4_txt.tabIndex = 5;
this.overview_btn.tabIndex = 6;
this.powerplant_btn.tabIndex = 7;
this.news_btn.tabIndex = 8;
this.safety_mc.tabIndex = 9;
this.text8_txt.tabIndex = 10;
this.text9_txt.tabIndex = 11;
this.bevel_mc.tabIndex = 12;
```

About testing your document with screen readers

You already know the importance of regularly testing your Flash document as you create it to ensure it performs as expected. Frequent testing is even more important when you design a document to work with assistive technologies such as screen readers. In addition to testing tab order in your SWF file, you should also test your tab order in various browsers; some browsers differ in how the user tabs to or out of Flash content. For information about resources to test your document with a screen reader, see "Testing accessible content" in Flash Help.

Summary

Congratulations on creating accessible Flash content. In a few minutes, you learned how to accomplish the following tasks:

- Specify that your document is accessible to screen readers
- Provide a document title and description
- Provide a title and description for document instances
- Specify that screen readers ignore elements in your document
- Change static text to dynamic text for accessibility
- Control the order in which users navigate with the Tab key
- Control the reading order with ActionScript

Macromedia maintains an extensive website devoted to accessibility. For more information about accessibility with Macromedia products, see the Macromedia accessibility website at www.macromedia.com/macromedia/accessibility.

Basic Tasks: Work with Layers

6

In Macromedia Flash Basic 8 and Macromedia Flash Professional 8, layers are analogous to transparent sheets of acetate stacked on top of each other. In the areas of a layer that don't contain content, you can see through to content in the layers below. Layers assist you in organizing content in your document. For example, you can keep background art on one layer and navigational buttons on another. Additionally, you can create and edit objects on one layer without affecting objects on another layer.

You can print this tutorial by downloading a PDF version of it from the Macromedia Flash Documentation page at www.macromedia.com/go/ fl_documentation.

In this tutorial, you will complete the following tasks:

Set up your workspace

First, you'll open the start file for the lesson and set up your workspace to use an optimal layout for taking lessons.

1. To open your start file, in Flash select File > Open and navigate to the file:

   - In Windows, browse to *boot drive*\Program Files\Macromedia\ Flash 8\Samples and Tutorials\Tutorial Assets\Basic Tasks\ Work with Layers and double-click layers_start.fla.

   - On the Macintosh, browse to *Macintosh HD*/Applications/ Macromedia Flash 8/Samples and Tutorials/Tutorial Assets/ Basic Tasks/Work with Layers and double-click layers_start.fla.

> **NOTE**
>
> The Work with Layers folder contains completed versions of the tutorial FLA files for your reference.

2. Select File > Save As and save the document with a new name, in the same folder, to preserve the original start file.

3. Select Window > Workspace Layout > Default to set up your workspace for taking lessons.

4. In the Stage View pop-up menu, in the upper-right side of the Timeline, select Show Frame to view both the Stage and the workspace.

5. If necessary, drag the lower edge of the Timeline (Window > Timeline) down to enlarge the Timeline view.

   You can also use the scroll bar to scroll through the layers.

Select a layer

You place objects, add text and graphics, and edit on the active layer. To make a layer active, you either select the layer in the Timeline or select a Stage object in the layer. The active layer is highlighted in the Timeline, and the pencil icon indicates it can be edited.

1. In the Tools panel, click the Selection tool.

2. On the Stage, select the red car.

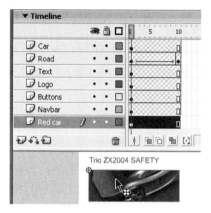

Trio ZX2004 SAFETY

A pencil icon in the Timeline indicates that the Red Car layer is now the active layer.

3. Select the Text layer in the Timeline.

    The text blocks above and below the red car are both selected on the Stage, since they're both on the Text layer.

Hide and show layers

You can hide layers to view content on other layers. When hiding layers, you have the option of hiding all layers in your document simultaneously or hiding layers individually.

1. Click the eye icon above the layers so that a red X appears in the Eye column.

   All content disappears from the Stage.

2. One by one, click each red X in the column and watch the content for the layer reappear on the Stage.

   Controls to the right of each layer name let you show or hide the contents of a layer.

NOTE	You may need to use the scroll bar to see all the layers.

Lock a layer

When you've placed content as desired on a layer, you can lock the layer to avoid inadvertent changes to the content by you or by others working on the document.

1. In the Timeline, click the black dot under the Lock column, next to the Logo layer.

   A padlock icon appears, indicating the layer is now locked.

2. With the Selection tool, try to drag the logo that appears along the top of the Stage.

   You can't drag the logo, because the layer is locked.

NOTE	If you accidentally drag something from an unlocked layer, press Control+Z (Windows) or Command+Z (Macintosh) to undo your change.

Add and name a layer

You'll now add a layer, name the layer, and then add a graphic symbol to the layer.

1. In the Timeline, click the Car layer.
2. Click Insert Layer below the Timeline.

   The new layer appears above the Car layer and becomes the active layer.
3. Double-click the layer name, type **Background** as the new name for the layer, and press Enter (Windows) or Return (Macintosh).

   As a best practice, always name each layer, and give the layer a meaningful name that indicates the type of content in the layer.
4. In the Library panel (Window > Library), select the background graphic symbol and drag it to the Stage.

   Because the Background layer is above all layers except the Mask layer, objects on that layer appear over objects on lower layers.

Change the order of layers

Obviously, you don't want the background to cover the other objects on the Stage. Normally, the background layer is the bottom layer on the Timeline. You'll move the Background layer you just created.

1. In the Timeline, drag the Background layer from the top position to the bottom position.

   All objects on the Stage now appear on top of the background.
2. With the Background layer still selected, in the Property inspector, enter 0 in the X text box and 72 in the Y text box. Press Enter (Windows) or Return (Macintosh) to precisely position the Background layer on the Stage.

Organize layers in a folder

You can create layer folders to organize layers and reduce Timeline clutter. The Timeline contains two layers that contain navigation objects: one for navigational buttons and another for navigational art. You'll create a layer folder, named Navigation, for both layers.

1. In the Timeline, select the Buttons layer.

 2. Click Insert Layer Folder, which is below the layer names.

 NOTE | If the Property inspector shows properties for the frame rather than for the movie clip, click the Background movie clip on the Stage.

3. Double-click the layer folder name and rename the folder **Navigation**.

4. Drag the Navbar layer and the Buttons layer to the Navigation folder.

   The layers appear indented to indicate that they're within the folder.

You can click the expander arrow to expand and collapse the folder and included layers.

Add a mask layer

Using a mask layer provides a simple way to selectively reveal portions of the layer or layers below it. Masking requires making one layer a mask layer and the layers below it masked layers.

You'll use the rectangular shape on the Stage to mask part of the road graphic and animation so that the animation fits better on the Stage.

1. On the Stage, with the Selection tool selected, click the rectangular shape below the road.

2. Drag the shape straight up and align the left edge of the shape with the left edge of the road.

3. Right-click (Windows) or Control-click (Macintosh) the Mask layer in the Timeline and select Mask from the context menu.

   The layer converts to a mask layer, indicated by a blue diamond-shaped icon. The layer immediately below the layer is linked to the mask layer. The masked layer's name is indented, and its icon changes to a blue layer icon.

4. In the Timeline, drag the Road layer to the Mask layer, placing it below the Car layer.

   The mask layer and the layers it masks are automatically locked.

5. To view the mask effect, select Control > Test Movie.

6. When you finish viewing the mask effect, close the SWF file window to return to your document.

Add a guide layer

So far you've learned about regular layers and mask layers. The third type of layer is a guide layer. You use guide layers to hold content that you don't want to appear in your published or exported file. For example, you could place instructions to others working on your document on a guide layer. As you take lessons in Flash, you'll notice that many of the lesson FLA files contain placeholders, which indicate where to place a Stage object, on guide layers. You'll create a guide layer now.

1. In the Timeline, select the Background layer and click Insert Layer to create a layer.

2. Name the new layer **Notes,** and press Enter (Windows) or Return (Macintosh).

3. Right-click (Windows) or Control-click (Macintosh) the Notes layer and select Guide from the context menu.

   An icon next to the layer name indicates that the layer is a guide layer.

4. With the Notes layer still selected, click the Text tool in the Tools panel. Then, in the area of the Stage above the car and road, enter **Production note: Animation with no stop (); actions loop by default.**

5. Save your document and select Control > Test Movie.

   No content that you added to the guide layer appears in the SWF file window.

6. When you finish viewing the SWF file, close the window to return to the document.

Delete a layer

Because you don't really need the guide layer in your document, you'll delete it.

- In the Timeline, with the Notes layer selected, click the Delete Layer button.

Summary

Congratulations on learning how to work with layers in Flash. In just a few minutes, you learned how to accomplish the following tasks:

- Select a layer.
- Hide and show layers.
- Lock a layer.
- Add and name a layer.
- Change the order of layers.
- Organize layers in a folder.
- Add a mask layer.
- Add a guide layer.
- Delete a layer.

To learn more about Flash, take another lesson.

CHAPTER 7

Basic Tasks: Create an Application

7

The application that you'll create in this lesson lets users view the cost of selecting multiple products. A Calculate button then adds the total cost.

You can print this tutorial by downloading a PDF version of it from the Macromedia Flash Documentation page at www.macromedia.com/go/ fl_documentation.

In this tutorial, you will complete the following tasks:

Set up your workspace

First, you'll open the start file for the lesson and set up your workspace to use an optimal layout for taking lessons.

1. To open your start file, in Flash select File > Open and navigate to the file:

   - In Windows, browse to *boot drive*\Program Files\Macromedia\ Flash 8\Samples and Tutorials\Tutorial Assets\Basic Tasks\ Create an Application and double-click calculator_start.fla.

   - On the Macintosh, browse to *Macintosh HD*/Applications/ Macromedia Flash 8/Samples and Tutorials/Tutorial Assets/ Basic Tasks/Create an Application and double-click calculator_start.fla.

   > **NOTE**
   > The Create an Application folder contains completed versions of the tutorial FLA files for your reference.

2. Select File > Save As and save the document with a new name, in the same folder, to preserve the original start file.

   > **NOTE**
   > As you complete this lesson, remember to save your work frequently.

3. Select Window > Workspace Layout > Default to set up your workspace for taking lessons.

   The form already includes an input text field in the QTY column and a dynamic text field in the Price column. You'll copy the text fields for the Shocks and Cover rows.

Copy input and dynamic text fields

You'll use input text fields to create a form.

1. Click the input text field where users enter the quantity of CD players. Press Alt and drag the copy of the field down to the Shocks QTY area.

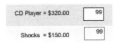

2. Alt-click the input text field that you just dragged; then drag the new copy of the field to the Cover QTY area.

3. Alt-click the dynamic text field for the CD player's price; then drag the copy of the field to the Shocks price area.

4. Alt-click the field that you just dragged; then drag the copy to the Cover price area.

Name text fields

Before you can specify values for the text fields in ActionScript, you first need to give each text field an instance name in the Property inspector. Appending the instance name with "txt" identifies the object as a text object.

1. Click the top input text field in the QTY column. In the Instance Name text box of the Property inspector (Window > Properties), type **qty1_txt**.

2. Follow the previous procedure to name the middle and bottom input text fields **qty2_txt** and **qty3_txt**, respectively.

3. Click the top dynamic text field in the Price column. In the Instance Name text box of the Property inspector, type **price1_txt**.

4. Follow the previous procedure to name the middle and bottom text fields in the column **price2_txt** and **price3_txt**, respectively.

Add and name a Button component

Components are movie clips that offer an easy way of adding advanced functionality to your document without having to know advanced ActionScript. You'll use the Button component to create a Calculate button that totals prices. Because the component you're using is based onv ActionScript 2.0, you first need to configure your Publish Settings dialog box to ensure your Flash content plays as expected.

1. Select File > Publish Settings.

2. On the Flash tab of the Publish Settings dialog box, select ActionScript 2.0 in the ActionScript Version pop-up menu, if it's not already selected.

3. In the Timeline, click the Components layer to select it.

4. From the Components panel (Window > Components), drag the Button component to the Stage and place it over the Calculate guide.

5. On the Parameters tab of the Property inspector, with the Button component selected, click the Button text on the Label row, and type **Calculate**. Then press Enter or Return.

   The text that you type in the Label text box is the text that appears on the component.

6. In the Instance Name text box, enter **calculate** to provide the button with an instance name.

Declare variables and values for the prices

For your application to multiply the quantity of parts selected by the price of the part, you need to define a variable for each part in ActionScript. The value for the variable is the cost of the part.

1. In the Timeline, click Frame 1 of the Actions layer and open the Actions panel (Window > Actions).

2. In the Script pane, type the following:

    ```
    // Declare variables and values for car part prices.
    ```

    The parallel slashes (//) indicate that the text that follows is a comment. As a best practice, always add comments that offer an explanation of your ActionScript.

> **NOTE**
>
> As you take this lesson, you might find that you'd like to turn off code hints—the tooltips that prompt you with the correct ActionScript syntax. If so, you can turn off code hinting by clicking the pop-up menu in the upper-right corner of the Actions panel. Select Preferences, and then deselect Code Hints on the ActionScript tab.

3. Press Enter (Windows) or Return (Macintosh) and type the following to indicate the cost of each part:

    ```
    var priceCD = 320;
    var priceShocks = 150;
    var priceCover = 125;
    ```

Specify values for input text fields

You must specify values for the input text fields. You'll use the values when you write ActionScript that multiplies the quantity and cost values.

1. In the Script pane, with the insertion point after the text that reads 125;, press Enter (Windows) or Return (Macintosh) twice and type the following:

    ```
    //Set initial values for the quantity text fields.
    ```

2. Press Enter or Return, and type the following:

    ```
    qty1_txt.text = 0;
    ```

    qty1_txt is the instance name that you gave the first input text field under the QTY column. The .text property defines the initial value in the text field, which you specify is 0.

3. Press Enter or Return, and type the following two lines to set values of 0 for the other two QTY fields:

    ```
    qty2_txt.text = 0;
    qty3_txt.text = 0;
    ```

    When you finish, the ActionScript should appear as follows:

    ```
    //Set initial values for the quantity text fields.
    qty1_txt.text = 0;
    qty2_txt.text = 0;
    qty3_txt.text = 0;
    ```

Write a function

A function is a script that you can use repeatedly to perform a specific task. You can pass parameters to a function, and it can return a value. In this lesson, every time your user clicks the Calculate button, a function will run that multiplies data in the input text fields and returns values in the dynamic text fields. You'll write that function now.

1. In the Script pane, with the insertion point after the ActionScript that reads `qty3_txt.text = 0;`, press Enter (Windows) or Return (Macintosh) twice and type the following comment:

   ```
   //Calculate quantity times price.
   ```

2. Press Enter or Return and type the following to create a function that runs when the playhead enters Frame 1, where you're attaching the script:

   ```
   this.onEnterFrame = function (){
   ```

3. Type the following ActionScript to specify how the function should multiply the values in the input text fields for the airplane:

   ```
   price1_txt.text = Number (qty1_txt.text)*Number
     (priceCD);
   ```

   `price1_txt` is the instance name that you gave to the top price input text field on the Stage.

   `.text` defines the text that should appear in the text field, which is the number of parts multiplied by the cost of the part: the $320 that you set as the value for the `priceCD` variable.

4. Press Enter or Return, and type the following two lines:

   ```
   price2_txt.text = Number (qty2_txt.text)*Number
     (priceShocks);
   price3_txt.text = Number (qty3_txt.text)*Number
     (priceCover);
   };
   ```

   Your function should appear as follows:

   ```
   //Calculate quantity times price.
   this.onEnterFrame = function (){
     price1_txt.text = Number (qty1_txt.text)*Number
     (priceCD);
     price2_txt.text = Number (qty2_txt.text)*Number
     (priceShocks);
     price3_txt.text = Number (qty3_txt.text)*Number
     (priceCover);
   };
   ```

Write an event handler for the component

For your SWF file to react to events such as a mouse click, you can use event handlers—ActionScript associated with a particular object and event. You'll use an `on()` event handler for the Button component that calculates the total price when users click the button.

For more information about event handlers, see "Handling Events" in Flash Help.

1. On the Stage, click the Button component and go to the Actions panel.

    The tab at the bottom of the Actions panel, labeled Calculate, indicates that you're attaching the script directly to the selected object rather than to a frame.

2. In the Script pane, type the following comment:

    ```
    //Calculates total price.
    ```

3. After the comment, press Enter (Windows) or Return (Macintosh) and type the following to create a handler for the PushButton component that you placed on the Stage:

    ```
    on(click) {
    ```

    You just typed the start of the `on()` event handler. The `(click)` specifies that the event should occur when the user clicks the Calculate button.

    A Button component has its own Timeline. In the Timeline hierarchy, the component Timeline is a child of the main Timeline. To point to elements from the Button component Timeline to the main Timeline in this script, you use the code `with (_parent)`.

4. With the insertion point at the end of the line you just typed, press Enter or Return and type the following:

    ```
    with(_parent){
    ```

5. Press Enter or Return and complete your handler by typing the following:

```
priceTotal_txt.text = Number (price1_txt.text) + Number
  (price2_txt.text) + Number (price3_txt.text);
  }
}
```

When you finish, your script should appear as follows:

```
on(click) {
  with(_parent){
  priceTotal_txt.text = Number (price1_txt.text) + Number
  (price2_txt.text) + Number (price3_txt.text);
  }
}
```

The event handler that you typed specifies that the text in the priceTotal_txt field should be the sum of the values in the price1_txt, price2_txt, and price3_txt fields.

Test your application

You'll test your application to ensure that it executes as expected.

1. Save your document and select Control > Test Movie.

2. In the test version of your movie that appears in Flash Player, type numbers in the QTY fields to see what appears in the Price fields.

3. Click Calculate to see the total price for all parts.

Summary

Congratulations on learning how to create an application. In a few minutes, you learned how to complete the following tasks:

- Copy input and dynamic text fields.
- Assign instance names to text fields.
- Add a Button component.
- Declare variables and values.
- Specify values for text fields.
- Write a function.
- Write an event handler for the component.

To learn more about ActionScript, see the ActionScript tutorials starting with Chapter 18, "ActionScript: Use Script Assist mode," on page 209.

CHAPTER 8

Basic Tasks: Use Layout Tools

Macromedia Flash Basic 8 and Macromedia Flash Professional 8 offer a variety of ways to place objects on the Stage. This tutorial teaches you how to use the layout tools in Flash to create a user interface.

You can print this tutorial by downloading a PDF version of it from the Macromedia Flash Documentation page at www.macromedia.com/go/ fl_documentation.

In this tutorial, you will complete the following tasks:

Although this lesson uses specific tools for particular types of objects (alignment guides to align text, for example), no strict rules exist about the best way to align a particular type of object. In your own projects, use whatever tools suit your needs.

Set up your workspace

First, you'll open the start file for the lesson and set up your workspace to use an optimal layout for taking lessons.

1. To open your start file, in Flash select File > Open and navigate to the file:

   - In Windows, browse to *boot drive*\Program Files\Macromedia\ Flash 8\Samples and Tutorials\Tutorial Assets\Basic Tasks\ Use Layout Tools and double-click layout_tools_start.fla.

   - On the Macintosh, browse to *Macintosh HD*/Applications/ Macromedia Flash 8/Samples and Tutorials/Tutorial Assets/ Basic Tasks/Use Layout Tools and double-click layout_tools_start.fla.

> **NOTE** The Use Layout Tools folder contains completed versions of the tutorial FLA files for your reference.

2. Select File > Save As and save the document with a new name, in the same folder, to preserve the original start file.

3. Select Window > Workspace Layout > Default to set up your workspace for taking lessons.

4. In the Stage View pop-up menu, in the upper-right side of the Timeline, select Show Frame to view both the Stage and the workspace.

5. Click in the workspace, away from objects on the Stage, so that no objects are selected.

Use guides to align an object

You can use rulers and guides to precisely position or align objects in your document. You'll add guides to help you center the block of text.

1. Select View > Rulers.

   A horizontal and vertical ruler appear above and to the left of the Stage.

2. Click anywhere in the horizontal ruler and drag down until you reach the 250-pixel horizontal position.

3. Click anywhere in the vertical ruler and drag left until you reach the 375-pixel vertical position.

4. Ensure that you have Snap to Guides turned on by selecting View > Snapping > Snap to Guides.

5. In the Tools panel, click the Selection tool.

6. On the Stage, click inside the upper-left corner of the blue text border and drag it to the intersection of the two guides.

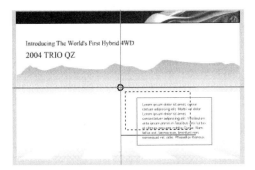

A small circle appears in the upper-left corner of the text border when you drag near the corner of the text border. The circle indicates that snapping is engaged.

7. If you want to remove the guides, select View > Guides > Clear Guides.

Change the Stage size

The Stage size of your document is 750 x 500 pixels. You'll change the Stage size to 640 x 480, a common size that supports a wide variety of screen sizes and resolutions.

1. Click in a blank area of the workspace to deselect the text block.

2. In the Property inspector, you see properties for the entire document. Click Size.

3. In the Document Properties dialog box, enter **640** for the width and **480** for the height, and click OK.

The document size changes, but the objects on the Stage remain the same size.

Resize objects to match the Stage size

When you changed the Stage size, art on the Stage extended off the Stage and into the workspace. You can easily resize the art to match the Stage size again.

1. On the Stage, click the gray mountains to select them. Shift-click the blue banner at the top of the Stage to add it to the selection.

2. Open the Align panel (Window > Align).

    Tooltips appear in the Align panel showing the names of alignment options.

3. In the Align panel, select To Stage; then, under Match Size, select Match Width. The size of the selected art changes to match the width of the Stage.

4. Still in the Align panel, click Align Left Edge.

    The art aligns to the left edge of the Stage.

5. In the Timeline, click the Bevel layer to select it.

6. From the Library panel (Window > Library), drag the bevel graphic to any area toward the bottom of the Stage.

7. In the Align panel, verify that To Stage is still selected, and click Match Width.

8. Click Align Left Edge and Align Bottom Edge.

    The bevel aligns to the bottom edge of the Stage.

9. Close the Library panel and the Align panel.

Specify snap alignment settings

Snapping offers a way of precisely placing an object on the Stage by having the object affix itself to other objects and alignment tools. You'll specify snap align settings to show horizontal and vertical guides, which will assist you in placing art on the Stage.

1. Select View > Snapping > Snap Align to set this option, if it is not already selected.

2. Select View > Snapping > Edit Snap Align.

3. In the Movie Border text box of the Snap Align dialog box, enter **30 px** (pixels) to snap objects to a 30-pixel Stage border.

4. Verify that 10 pixels appears in both the Horizontal and Vertical Snap Tolerance text boxes.

   Snap tolerance determines how close an object must be to another object or alignment tool before it snaps into place.

5. Click OK.

Align an object using the alignment guides

Now that you've specified snap alignment settings, you'll use the snap alignment settings that you specified to assist you in placing an object on the Stage.

1. In the Tools panel, click the Selection tool.

2. In the Timeline, select the Auto layer.

3. From the Library panel (Window > Library), drag the auto graphic and place it on the Stage, anywhere in the gray area next to the body text.

4. Drag the auto instance again so that the snap alignment guides appear. Move the car close to the body text, and up and down as necessary until the center alignment guide appears. The guide indicates the auto is centered in relation to the body text.

5. While keeping the car centered with the body text (you should continue to see the center alignment guide), drag the auto in a straight line, toward the left of the Stage, until the guide snaps at the 30-pixel border that you created previously.

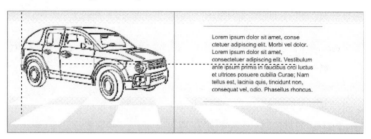

You've aligned the car with the text as well as to the snapping border.

Align objects using the Align panel

Previously, you used the Align panel to match objects to the size of the Stage. Now you'll use the Align panel to center objects in relation to each other, and in relation to the Stage.

1. With the Selection tool, click the text on the Stage that reads "Introducing the World's First Hybrid 4WD."

2. Shift-click the second line of title text, "2004 Trio QZ," to add it to the selection.

3. In the Align panel (Window > Align), deselect To Stage and select Align Horizontal Center.

   You've centered the two rows in relation to their horizontal axes. Next, you'll group the title text to center both lines in relation to the Stage.

4. With both lines of text still selected, select Modify > Group.

5. In the Align panel, select To Stage, and then select Align Horizontal Center again.

   With To Stage selected, the objects align in relation to the horizontal center of the Stage.

6. Close the Align panel.

Snap objects to each other

You can snap objects on the Stage to other objects on the Stage, thereby setting the alignment of objects to each other. Using the Snap to Objects feature, you'll align a navigation bar with the top Stage banner.

1. Select View > Snapping. In the submenu, select Snap to Objects if it's not already selected.

2. In the Timeline, select the Nav layer.

3. From the Library panel, drag the nav graphic to any area of the Stage below the blue banner, and then release the nav graphic.

4. Click the upper-left corner of the nav graphic, and drag it so that a circular snap indicator appears.

5. With the snap indicator visible, drag the upper-left corner of the nav bar and snap it into place against the lower-left corner of the blue banner.

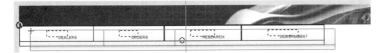

Align objects using the Property inspector

The Property inspector lets you precisely align objects on the *x* and *y* Stage axes, from the registration point of the Stage object. The registration point is the point from which a symbol aligns or rotates. You'll use the Property inspector to align the logo.

1. In the Timeline, select the Top layer.

2. From the Library panel (Window > Library), drag the logo to an empty area of the Stage.

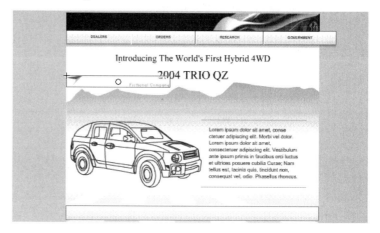

3. In the Property inspector, with the logo still selected, enter **20** in the X text box and **8** in the Y text box. Press Enter (Windows) or Return (Macintosh).

   The logo moves to the new *x* and *y* Stage values.

> **NOTE**
> You can view and change the registration point of an object in the Info panel (Window > Info). The black square in the grid represents the registration point. To change it, you click another square in the grid.

Align objects using the grid and arrow keys

You can use the grid to assist you in placing objects on the Stage.

1. Select View > Grid > Show Grid.

   The grid does not appear when you test or publish your document.

> **NOTE**
> If you wanted to snap objects to the horizontal and vertical grid lines, you would also select Snap to Grid (View > Snapping > Snap to Grid). For this lesson, you won't snap objects to the grid.

2. On the Stage, select the title text you previously grouped together.

3. Use the Up Arrow key on your keyboard to nudge the text until the first line in the title text is on a horizontal grid line. Be sure to leave space between the title text and the navigation bar.

> **NOTE**
> You can also use the Left Arrow, Down Arrow, and Right Arrow keys to nudge objects on the Stage in the direction of the arrow.

Summary

Congratulations on using layout tools to create a user interface. In a few minutes, you learned how to accomplish the following tasks:

- View the workspace rulers
- Use guides to align objects
- Change the Stage size
- Resize objects to match the Stage size
- Align an object using the alignment guides
- Snap objects to each other
- Align objects using the Property inspector
- Use the grid and arrow keys to align objects

For more information about design topics in Flash, take another lesson from the Basic Tasks series.

CHAPTER 9

Basic Tasks: Create Symbols and Instances

9

A symbol is a reusable object, and an instance is an occurrence of a symbol on the Stage. Repeatedly using instances does not increase the file size and is a good part of a strategy for keeping a document file size small. Symbols also simplify editing a document; when you edit a symbol, all instances of the symbol update to reflect the edits. Another benefit of symbols is that they allow you to create sophisticated interactivity.

You can print this tutorial by downloading a PDF version of it from the Macromedia Flash Documentation page at www.macromedia.com/go/fl_documentation.

In this tutorial, you will complete the following tasks:

Set up your workspace

First, you'll open the start file for the lesson and set up your workspace to use an optimal layout for taking lessons.

1. To open your start file, in Flash select File > Open and navigate to the file:

    - In Windows, browse to *boot drive*\Program Files\Macromedia\ Flash 8\Samples and Tutorials\Tutorial Assets\Basic Tasks\ Create Symbols and Instances and double-click symbols_start.fla.

    - On the Macintosh, browse to *Macintosh HD*/Applications/ Macromedia Flash 8/Samples and Tutorials/Tutorial Assets/ Basic Tasks/Create Symbols and Instances and double-click symbols_start.fla.

> **NOTE** The Create Symbols and Instances folder contains completed versions of the tutorial FLA files for your reference.

    The document opens in the Flash authoring environment.

2. Select File > Save As and save the document with a new name, in the same folder, to preserve the original start file.

    As you complete this lesson, remember to save your work frequently.

3. Select Window > Workspace Layout > Default to configure your workspace.

About creating symbols

When you create a symbol, you specify one of the following symbol behaviors:

- Graphic
- Movie clip
- Button

In this lesson, you'll work with graphic and movie clip symbols. For a lesson about button symbols, select Help > Flash Tutorials > Basic Tasks: Add Button Animation and Navigation.

Create a graphic symbol

A graphic symbol is well suited for repeated use of static images, or for creating animations associated with the main Timeline. Unlike with movie clip and button symbols, you cannot give instance names to graphic symbols, nor can you refer to them in ActionScript.

You'll take vector art on the Stage and turn it into a graphic symbol.

1. In the Tools panel, click the Selection tool.
2. On the Stage, drag around the car to select it.

3. Select Modify > Convert to Symbol.
4. In the Convert to Symbol dialog box, enter **CarGraphic** as the name and select Graphic as the behavior.
5. The Registration grid uses a small black square to indicate where, within the symbol bounding box, the registration point is located. A registration point is the axis around which the symbol rotates, and the point along which the symbol aligns. Click the upper-left square on the grid to select the registration point location, and click OK.
6. The car on the Stage is now an instance of the CarGraphic symbol. The Property inspector shows properties for the graphic symbol instance.

7. Open the Library panel (Window > Library) to view the symbol.

   You'll find the CarGraphic symbol in the Library panel. Flash stores symbols in the library. Each document has its own library, and you can share libraries between different FLA files.

Duplicate and modify an instance of a symbol

After you've created a symbol, you can use instances of it repeatedly in your document. You can modify the following instance properties for an individual instance without affecting other instances or the original symbol: color, scale, rotation, alpha transparency, brightness, tint, height, width, and location.

If you edit the symbol later, the instance retains its modified properties in addition to acquiring the symbol edits.

You'll now duplicate the instance of the car, and change the tint for the duplicate.

1. On the Stage, select the car. Press Alt and drag the car up to create another instance.

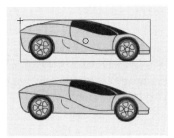

2. With the duplicate selected, select Tint from the Color pop-up menu in the Property inspector.

3. In the RGB area, enter **0** in the Red Color pop-up menu, **0** in the Green Color pop-up menu, and **255** in the Blue Color pop-up menu. Then press Enter (Windows) or Return (Macintosh).

    The duplicate instance turns blue, but the original instance remains unchanged.

Modify a symbol

You can enter symbol-editing mode by double-clicking any instance of a symbol. Changes that you make in symbol-editing mode affect all instances of the symbol.

1. Do one of the following to enter symbol-editing mode:

   ▪ On the Stage, double-click one of the car instances.

   ▪ In the Library panel, double-click the CarGraphic symbol.

   Next to Scene 1 toward the top of the workspace, the name of the symbol appears, which indicates that you're in symbol-editing mode for the named symbol.

2. In the Tools panel, select the Free Transform tool and drag around the bottom car to select the entire car.

   In symbol-editing mode, the car is a graphic, within a symbol, that you can manipulate as you would any other vector graphic.

3. Drag the middle-right sizing handle of the Free Transform tool slightly to the right to stretch the symbol.

   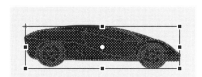

4. Click Scene 1, above the Timeline, to exit symbol-editing mode.

   Both instances of the symbol reflect the transformation.

Create a movie clip symbol

A movie clip symbol is analogous in many ways to a document within a document. This symbol type has its own Timeline independent of the main Timeline. You can add movie clips within other movie clips and buttons to create nested movie clips. You can also use the Property inspector to assign an instance name to an instance of a movie clip, and then reference the instance name in ActionScript.

You'll convert the tire on the Stage into a movie clip.

1. With the Selection tool, click the tire on the Stage to select it and select Modify > Convert to Symbol.

2. In the Convert to Symbol dialog box, enter **MCWheel** as the name, and select MovieClip as the behavior.

3. In the Registration grid, this time select the center square as the registration point, so the center of the movie clip becomes the axis around which the symbol rotates. Click OK.

   The image on the Stage is now an instance of the **MCWheel** symbol in the library.

Assign an instance name to the movie clip

To refer to an instance in ActionScript, and as a general best practice, always assign instance names to buttons and movie clip symbols. (You cannot assign an instance name to a graphic symbol.)

- In the Property inspector, with the instance of MCWheel selected on the Stage, enter **wheel_mc** in the Instance Name text box.

Add an effect to the movie clip

You can create an animation within a movie clip Timeline, in symbol-editing mode, that plays independent of the main Timeline. You'll add an effect to the MCWheel symbol that will cause all instances of the symbol to spin.

1. With the Selection tool, double-click the wheel_mc instance to enter symbol-editing mode.

2. Right-click (Windows) or Control-click (Macintosh) the symbol and select Timeline Effects > Transform/Transition > Transform.

3. In the Transform dialog box, enter **60** in the Effect Duration text box to specify that the effect spans 60 frames in the Timeline.

4. In the Spin text box, enter **1** and verify that 360 populates the Rotate text box.

5. Click Update Preview to view a preview of the effect and click OK.

   The effect spans 60 frames in the movie clip Timeline.

6. Click Scene 1 above the Timeline to exit symbol-editing mode.

7. Select Control > Test Movie to view the animation.

Summary

Congratulations on learning about symbols and instances. In a few minutes, you accomplished the following tasks:

- Create a graphic symbol.
- Duplicate and modify an instance.
- Create a movie clip symbol.
- Edit a symbol by adding an effect.

To learn more about Flash, take another lesson in the Basic Tasks series.

CHAPTER 10

Basic Tasks: Add Button Animation and Navigation

10

A *button* is a symbol that contains special frames for different button states, such as when the user's mouse pointer is over the button or when the user clicks the button. When you select the Button behavior for a new symbol, Macromedia Flash Basic 8 and Macromedia Flash Professional 8 create the Timeline for the button states. You can add navigation to buttons by using behaviors or by writing ActionScript.

This tutorial teaches you about creating and modifying buttons, including adding animation to a button.

You can print this tutorial by downloading a PDF version of it from the Macromedia Flash Documentation page at www.macromedia.com/go/ fl_documentation.

In this tutorial, you will complete the following tasks:

If you are not familiar with symbols and instances, before taking this lesson select Help > How Do I > Basic Flash > Create Symbols and Instances to take that lesson.

Set up your workspace

First, you'll open the start file for the lesson and set up your workspace to use an optimal layout for taking lessons.

1. To open your start file, in Flash select File > Open and navigate to the file:

   - In Windows, browse to *boot drive*\Program Files\Macromedia\ Flash 8\Samples and Tutorials\Tutorial Assets\Basic Tasks\ Add Button Animation and Navigation and double-click buttons_start.fla.

   - On the Macintosh, browse to *Macintosh HD*/Applications/ Macromedia Flash 8/Samples and Tutorials/Tutorial Assets/ Basic Tasks/Add Button Animation and Navigation and double-click buttons_start.fla.

> **NOTE** The Add Button Animation and Navigation folder contains completed versions of the tutorial FLA files for your reference.

2. Select File > Save As and save the document with a new name, in the same folder, to preserve the original start file.

3. Select Window > Workspace Layout > Default to set up your workspace for taking lessons.

4. In the Stage View pop-up menu, in the upper-right side of the Timeline, select Show Frame to view both the Stage and the workspace.

5. Click in the workspace, away from objects on the Stage, so that no objects are selected.

Create a button from grouped objects

You can create buttons from text and graphics, including bitmap images and grouped objects. In this lesson, you'll turn a logo and some text into one large button.

1. In the Tools panel, click the Selection tool. On the Stage, select the grouped text and logo, and then select Modify > Convert to Symbol.

2. In the Convert to Symbol dialog box, name the symbol **BTNLogo**, and select Button as the behavior.

3. In the Registration grid, verify that the square in the upper-left corner is selected as the registration point, and click OK.

   The registration point is the point from which the symbol aligns and rotates.

Name a button instance

As a best practice, you should name instances of symbols on the Stage. ActionScript relies on the instance name to identify the object.

■ With the button that you created still selected, open the Property inspector (Window > Properties). In the Instance Name text box, type **logo_btn**.

View the hit area by enabling buttons

When the Enable Simple Buttons feature is active, you can view the less complex aspects of your buttons, such as the hit area (the clickable area of a button) and the colors used for the button states. More complex button design, such as animation, does not play.

1. Click in an empty space in the workspace to make sure you don't have any objects selected.

2. Select Control > Enable Simple Buttons, and move the mouse pointer over different areas of the button that you created.

   The only areas of the button that are clickable (as indicated when the pointer changes to a hand) are the text area and the logo. The white space around the text and logo are not clickable.

3. Select Control > Enable Simple Buttons again to deselect the feature so that you can edit the button.

Next, you'll redefine the hit area so that the button area covers the entire grouped area.

Change the hit area of a button

You can specify a hit area that's a different size from the default hit area by adding a keyframe to the Hit frame of the button symbol, and then drawing a shape that defines the hit area.

1. On the Stage, double-click the logo button that you created to view the button Timeline. The button Timeline contains the following states:
   - Up
   - Over
   - Down
   - Hit

2. Double-click the Layer 1 name in the Timeline and rename the layer **Hit Area**.

3. Select the Hit frame (Frame 4) of the Hit Area layer in the BTNLogo Timeline, and press F6 to add a keyframe.

4. In the Tools panel, select the Rectangle tool. The stroke and fill color for the rectangle are unimportant. On the Stage, draw a rectangle that covers, as closely as possible, the logo and text.

The rectangle now defines the clickable area of the button.

5. Click Scene 1, above the upper-left side of the Stage, to exit symbol-editing mode for the button.

6. Select Control > Enable Simple Buttons.

7. On the Stage, again move the pointer over the text.

   The hit area changes to the shape of the rectangle that you drew.

8. Select Control > Enable Simple Buttons to deselect that feature.

Align buttons

You can align buttons along horizontal and vertical axes using the Align panel.

1. In the Timeline, click the Content layer.

2. Click Insert Layer below the Timeline.

3. Double-click the layer name, type **Animated Buttons** as the new name for the layer, and press Enter (Windows) or Return (Macintosh).

4. In the Library panel (Window > Library) select Button 1 and drag it to the lower-right edge of the Stage. Precise placement isn't necessary.

5. In the Instance Name text box in the Property inspector, give the button the instance name **links_btn**.

6. Drag Button 2 and Button 3 from the Library panel, placing them to the left of Button 1. Use the approximate spacing shown in the following illustration:

7. Using the Selection tool, drag to select all three buttons.

8. Open the Align panel by selecting Window > Align. Verify that To Stage is not selected, because you do not want to align the buttons relative to the Stage.

9. In the Align panel, click Align Vertical Center, and then click Distribute Horizontal Center.

   The buttons align on the Stage.

10. Close the Align panel.

11. On the Stage, click in an empty space in the workspace to make sure you don't have any objects selected, and select Button 2. In the Instance Name text box in the Property inspector, enter **contact_btn**. Select Button 3 and name it **sweepstakes_btn**.

Create animation for a button state

You'll create a movie clip within the Over state of Button 1, and create a shape tween in the movie clip. The shape tween creates an effect that changes the color from gray to red.

1. On the Stage, double-click Button 1 to open it in symbol-editing mode.

2. In the Button 1 Timeline, hide all layers except the Color layer. In the Color layer, select the Over keyframe.

NOTE | You hide layers by clicking the dot under the Eye column next to the layer name so that a red X appears.

3. On the Stage, select the black oval shape for Button 1. Press F8 to make the oval a symbol.

4. In the Convert to Symbol dialog box, name the symbol **Button Animation**. Select Movie Clip (not Button) as the behavior and click OK.

5. On the Stage, double-click the Button Animation symbol to switch to symbol-editing mode.

6. Rename Layer 1 to **Color Change**. Select Frame 15 and press F6 to add a keyframe.

7. With the playhead still on Frame 15, select the button shape on the Stage, and in the Property inspector select a bright shade of red from the Fill Color pop-up menu.

8. In the Timeline, click any frame between Frames 1 and 15. In the Property inspector, select Shape from the Tween pop-up menu.

   Drag the playhead from Frames 1 to 15 to see the color change.

Add an action to a button

When the user clicks the button and the tweened animation plays, you want the playhead to move to the end of the Button Animation Timeline and then stop. You'll use ActionScript to control playhead movement in a Timeline.

1. Add a new layer to the Button Animation Timeline and name it **Actions**.

2. On the Actions layer, add a keyframe to Frame 15 by pressing F6.

3. Open the Actions panel (Window > Actions) and if necessary, enlarge it to view both the Actions toolbox and the Script pane.

4. With Frame 15 of the Actions layer selected, go to the Global Functions > Timeline Control category of the Actions toolbox and double-click `stop`.

   The `stop` action lets you specify that the playhead stop when it reaches Frame 15.

   In the Button Animation Timeline, Frame 15 of the Actions layer now displays a small *a,* which indicates that an action is attached to that frame.

5. Click Scene 1, above the Stage, to exit symbol-editing mode and return to the main document.

6. Click the pop-up menu control in the upper-right side of the Actions panel, and select Close Panel.

7. Select Control > Enable Simple Buttons so you can test the animated button.

8. On the Stage, move the pointer over the button and click the button.

9. Select Control > Enable Simple Buttons to deselect that feature.

Add navigation to a button

With behaviors, you can quickly add navigation to a button without having to know ActionScript. You'll add navigation to open a web page when the user clicks a button.

1. On the Stage, select the instance of Button 1.

2. In the Behaviors panel (Window > Behaviors), click Add Behavior and select Web > Go to Web Page.

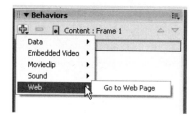

3. In the Go to URL dialog box, select _blank in the Open In pop-up menu to open the URL in a new browser window. In the URL text box, either accept the default setting of http://www.macromedia.com or enter a different URL. Click OK.

4. If desired, repeat the previous steps, selecting Button 2 and then Button 3, to add navigation to those buttons as well.

5. Click the pop-up menu control in the upper-right side of the Behavior panel, and select Close Panel.

Test the SWF file

You'll test your document to view the button animation and see if the navigation works as expected.

1. Save your document and select Control > Test Movie.

2. Move the mouse pointer over the instance of Button 1 to view the color animation that you created.

3. Click the button to see if your web browser opens to the URL that you specified.

4. If you added navigation to the other two buttons, test those buttons as well.

5. When you finish viewing the SWF file, close the SWF file and web browser windows.

Summary

Congratulations on learning about buttons. In a few minutes, you were able to accomplish the following tasks:

- Create a button from grouped objects.
- Name a button instance.
- View the hit area of a button.
- Change the hit area of a button.
- Align buttons.
- Create animation for a button state.
- Add an action to a button.
- Add navigation to a button.

To learn more about Flash, take another lesson.

CHAPTER 11

Basic Tasks: Create a Presentation with Screens (Flash Professional Only)

11

Flash Professional 8 offers a new way to create presentations with slide screens. If you can imagine placing media on slide screens, adding nested slides that inherit media from other slides, and using the built-in controls to navigate through the slides at runtime, you've imagined exactly how easy it is to create a presentation with slide screens.

You can print this tutorial by downloading a PDF version of it from the Macromedia Flash Documentation page at www.macromedia.com/go/fl_documentation.

In this tutorial, you will complete the following tasks:

Set up your workspace

First, you'll open the start file for the lesson and set up your workspace to use an optimal layout for taking lessons.

1. To open your start file, in Flash select File > Open and navigate to the file:

   - In Windows, browse to *boot drive*\Program Files\Macromedia\ Flash 8\Samples and Tutorials\Tutorial Assets\Basic Tasks\ Presentation with Screens and double-click presentation_start.fla.

   - On the Macintosh, browse to *Macintosh HD*/Applications/ Macromedia Flash 8/Samples and Tutorials/Tutorial Assets/ Basic Tasks/Presentation with Screens and double-click presentation_start.fla.

   > **NOTE**
   > The Presentation with Screens folder contains completed versions of the tutorial FLA files for your reference.

   The document opens in the Flash authoring environment.

2. Select File > Save As and save the document with a new name, in the same folder, to preserve the original start file.

   As you complete this lesson, remember to save your work frequently.

3. Select Window > Workspace Layout > Default to configure your workspace.

View the screen hierarchy and screen Timelines

You add content to screens in much the same way that you add content to the Stage, but screens are nested movie clips, relying on a hierarchy, nested timelines, and inheritance. All screens exist in the first frame of the root timeline, which is hidden, and all screen content loads on the first frame. For more information about screens, see "Working with Screens (Flash Professional Only)" in Flash Help.

1. If the Screen Outline pane is not visible, select Window > Other Panels > Screens.

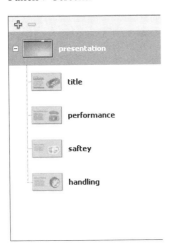

The Screen Outline pane displays a thumbnail view of each slide in the presentation, and the presentation hierarchy.

When you select a screen in the Screen Outline pane, the screen appears in the Document window. When you select multiple screens, the content of the first screen selected appears in the Document window.

2. In the Screen Outline pane, select the presentation screen.

All slide screen documents contain a presentation screen, which is at the top level of the screen hierarchy. Think of the presentation slide as a master slide: content on the presentation slide can appear in all slides in your document.

The four slides that appear indented beneath the presentation slide in the pane represent nested, or child, screens, and the presentation slide is the parent.

3. Open the Timeline, if it's not already open (Window > Timeline). Select another slide in the Screen Outline pane to view the Timeline for that screen.

Each screen has its own Timeline. The main Timeline for a document with screens, however, is never visible.

View screen properties

You can view different properties for a slide, depending on where you select the slide.

1. In the Screen Outline pane, select the presentation thumbnail.

The Property inspector allows you to change the instance name, which is also the name of the screen as it appears in the Screen Outline pane.

2. Select the actual presentation slide, not the thumbnail.

The Property inspector now displays the same controls you're probably used to when working with the Stage and document properties.

Add content to a presentation slide

You'll add navigation buttons to the presentation slide so that the buttons appear on each slide in the presentation.

1. In the Screen Outline pane, select the presentation slide thumbnail. In the Timeline, select Frame 1 of the Navigation layer.

2. From the Library panel, drag the *NextBtn* symbol to the screen, placing it within the black band at the bottom of the screen.

3. In the Property inspector, with the button still selected, enter **280** in the X text box and **165** in the Y text box to place the button.

> **NOTE**
> The coordinates that you enter are in relation to the default center registration point of the slide. For more information about the registration point in screens, see "Specifying the ActionScript class and registration point of a screen (Flash Professional only)" in Flash Help.

4. Enter **forwardBtn** in the Instance Name text box.

5. Drag *PrevBtn* to the slide and use the Property inspector to enter **245** in the X text box and **165** in the Y text box.

6. Enter **backBtn** in the Instance Name text box.

7. In the Screen Outline pane, select each nested slide to verify that the buttons now appear on all slides.

> **NOTE**
> Content on a parent screen appears slightly dimmed when you view it on a nested screen.

Add screen navigation behaviors to buttons

When you open a new Flash Slide Presentation, the document already includes functionality that lets users navigate between slide screens using the keyboard arrow keys. You'll also add navigation behaviors to the buttons, offering users an additional option to navigate between slides.

> **NOTE** By default, keyboard arrow keys let you navigate between screens on the same level, not between nested screens.

1. On the presentation slide, select the forwardBtn instance. In the Behaviors panel (Window > Behaviors) click Add (+), and then select Screen > Go to Next Slide from the menu.

2. On the presentation slide, select the backBtn instance. In the Behaviors panel (Window > Behaviors) click Add (+), and then select Screen > Go to Previous Slide from the menu.

3. Select Control > Test Movie, and click the buttons in the SWF file window that appears. You want to make sure your buttons function as expected. When you finish testing your document, close the SWF file window.

Add and name a slide

You can easily add slides to your presentation using the context menu in the Screen Outline pane.

1. In the Screen Outline pane, select the title thumbnail. Right-click (Windows) or Control-click (Macintosh) and select Insert Screen from the context menu.

A new screen appears in the Screen Outline pane, at the same level as the title slide. The new slide automatically inherits media from the presentation slide.

2. Double-click the new slide's name in the Screen Outline pane, and name the slide **features**.

Select and move slides

You can copy, cut, paste, and drag screens in the Screen Outline pane to change their order in the presentation. You'll select three screens, cut them, and paste them so that they're nested as children of the features slide.

1. In the Screen Outline pane, select the performance slide. Shift-click the safety and handling slides to add them to the selection.

2. Right-click (Windows) or Control-click (Macintosh) the selected slides and select Cut from the context menu.

3. In the Screen Outline pane, right-click (Windows) or Control-click (Macintosh) the features slide and select Paste Nested Screen from the context menu.

    The three slides now appear as children of the features slide.

Add content to a new slide

The features slide, as a child of the presentation slide, inherits properties from that slide. Additionally, because the features slide is a parent to the three slides that you copied and pasted, content that you add to that slide appears on the three children slides.

1. In the Screen Outline pane, select the features thumbnail. From the Library panel, drag the Features Content symbol to anywhere in the Document window.

2. In the Property inspector, give the instance of Features Content an instance name of **features_mc**.

3. In the Property inspector, enter **-275** in the X text box and **-130** in the Y text box to place the instance.

Add transition behaviors

Although your presentation is fairly complete, you'll add transition behaviors to make the presentation more interesting. Specifically, you'll add behaviors that make content fade and appear to fly off the Document window.

1. In the Screen Outline pane, select the features slide. In the Behaviors panel, click Add (+) and select Screen > Transition from the menu.

2. In the Transitions dialog box, select Fade from the list of transitions and view the preview in the lower-left side of the dialog box. Verify that 2 seconds is selected as the duration and that In is selected as the direction, and then click OK.

3. In the Behaviors panel, click Reveal in the Event column to open the pop-up menu and select revealChild. The revealChild option specifies that the behavior will reveal the next child screen.

4. To add the Fly behavior, verify that the features slide is still selected. In the Behaviors panel, click Add (+) and select Screen > Transition from the menu.

5. In the Transitions dialog box, select Fly from the list of transitions, and select Out as the direction.

6. In the Duration text box, enter .5 as the length of time to complete the transition.

7. In the Start Location pop-up menu, select Left Center and watch the transition preview, and then click OK.

   In the Behaviors panel, revealChild now appears twice. With the Fly behavior, however, you want to hide the child screen.

8. In the Behaviors panel, click the second event in the list, which is the one you just added. In the pop-up menu, select hideChild.

Event	Action
revealChild	Transition...
hideChild	Transition...

Test your presentation

Your presentation is now complete and ready to test.

1. Select Control > Test Movie.

2. Use the Forward and Backward navigation buttons to move through the presentation and view the transitions.

Summary

Congratulations on learning how to create a slide presentation with screens. In a few minutes, you learned how to accomplish the following tasks:

- Add content to a presentation slide.
- Add screen navigation to buttons.
- Add and name a slide.
- Select and move slides.
- Add content to a new slide.
- Add transition behaviors to a slide.

To learn more about using screens, see "Working with Screens (Flash Professional Only)" in Flash Help.

CHAPTER 12

Creating Graphics: Draw in Flash

12

When you draw in Flash, you create vector art, which is a mathematical representation of lines, curves, color, and position. Vector art is resolution-independent; you can rescale the art to any size or display it at any resolution without losing clarity. Additionally, vector art downloads faster than comparable bitmap images. This tutorial shows you how to create vector art of a bolt and logo.

You can print this tutorial by downloading a PDF version of it from the Macromedia Flash Documentation page at www.macromedia.com/go/fl_documentation.

In this tutorial, you will complete the following tasks:

Set up your workspace

First, you'll open the start file for the lesson and set up your workspace to use an optimal layout for taking lessons.

1. To open your start file, in Flash select File > Open and navigate to the file:

   - In Windows, browse to *boot drive*\Program Files \Macromedia\ Flash 8\Samples and Tutorials\Tutorial Assets\ Creating Graphics\Draw in Flash and double-click drawing_start.fla.

   - On the Macintosh, browse to *Macintosh HD*/Applications/ Macromedia Flash 8/Samples and Tutorials/Tutorial Assets/ Creating Graphics/Draw in Flash and double-click drawing_start.fla.

> **NOTE** The Draw in Flash folder contains completed versions of the tutorial FLA files for your reference.

   Flash opens in the authoring environment.

2. Select File > Save As and save the document with a new name, in the same folder, to preserve the original start file.

   As you complete this lesson, remember to save your work frequently.

3. Select Window > Workspace Layout > Default to configure your workspace.

Select a shape tool

Shape tools offer an easy way to create figures such as ovals, rectangles, polygons, and stars. You'll use the PolyStar tool to create a polygon.

1. In the Timeline, select the Content layer.

2. In the Tools panel, select the PolyStar tool. You may need to click the lower-right control on the Rectangle tool to see a menu that displays the PolyStar tool.

3. Click anywhere in the gray workspace beside the Stage to display properties for the shape you'll create. In the Property inspector (Window > Properties), verify that black is selected as the stroke color, 1 pixel is selected as the stroke height, and Solid is selected as the stroke style.

   The stroke is the line that outlines your shape.

4. Click the Fill Color control and select blue with a hexadecimal value of #0000FF.

   The fill color appears within the stroke in a shape.

Select options to create a polygon

The PolyStar tool offers options that let you specify the number of sides in a polygon; you can also use options for the tool to create a star. You'll specify that your polygon has six sides.

1. In the Property inspector, with the PolyStar tool still selected, click Options.

2. In the Tools Setting dialog box, verify that Polygon appears in the Style pop-up menu, and then enter **6** in the Number of Sides text box. Click OK.

Draw a polygon

Pressing Shift constrains your shape along a vertical or horizontal line.

■ Press Shift and drag over the left side of the Stage (away from the numbers on the Guides layer) to draw a hexagon, as shown in the following illustration:

Rotate the shape

After you've created a shape, you can use the Transform panel to specify a precise number of degrees in which to rotate the shape.

1. In the Tools panel, click the Selection tool. On the Stage, double-click within the hexagon to select both the stroke and the fill.

   Clicking once within a shape selects only the fill.

2. Select Window > Transform. In the Transform dialog box, verify that Rotate is selected, and enter -15 in the Rotate text box to rotate the shape 15° clockwise. Press Enter (Windows) or Return (Macintosh).

Use the cutout feature

When you create one shape on top of another on the same layer, and the two shapes are ungrouped, the shape on top "cuts out" the area of the shape underneath. You'll create a circle within the hexagon and then cut out the circle.

1. Select View > Snapping and select Snap to Objects if it's not already selected.

2. In the Tools panel, click the Oval tool. While pressing Shift to constrain the shape, draw a circle within the hexagon (imagine the hexagon as the face of a clock and begin your circle at the 10:00 corner point, dragging to the 4:00 corner point), as in the following illustration.

> NOTE
> If you make an error drawing the circle, press Control+Z (Windows) or Command+Z (Macintosh) to undo your circle.

3. In the Tools panel, click the Selection tool. On the Stage, click within the circle, and press Backspace or Delete.

Transform the shape of your drawing

Using the Free Transform tool, you can scale, rotate, compress, stretch, or skew lines and shapes. You'll use the Free Transform tool to compress your drawing.

1. In the Tools panel, select the Free Transform tool. Double-click the hexagon on the Stage to select both the stroke and the fill.

2. Drag the upper-middle handle of the Free Transform tool down to transform the hexagon into the following shape:

Copy strokes

You can select and copy strokes, which you'll do now to create the lower edge of the bolt.

1. With the Selection tool, click anywhere on the Stage or workspace, away from an object, to deselect the shape.

2. Shift-click the three lines of the shape on the Stage that comprise the bottom of the hexagon to select them, as shown in the following illustration:

3. Press Shift+Alt and drag down slightly to drag a copy of the three lines, as in the following illustration:

Draw with the Line tool

The Line tool allows you to draw straight lines in any direction.

■ In the Tools panel, select the Line tool. On the Stage, draw four vertical lines from the hexagon to the stroke copies that you dragged down, as shown in the following illustration:

Select and add a different fill color

You can use the Paint Bucket tool to change an existing color and to fill empty areas surrounded by lines. You'll use the Paint Bucket tool to add a fill color to the empty areas of your drawing.

1. In the Tools panel, select the Paint Bucket tool. In the colors area, click the Fill Color control and select blue with the hexadecimal value of #3366FF.

2. On the Stage, click within the lines to add the selected color to the empty areas, as shown in the following illustration:

Group the shape

You can manipulate the stroke and fill of a shape as separate entities, as you did earlier, or you can group the stroke with the fill to manipulate the shape as a single graphic, which you'll do now.

1. With the Selection tool, drag around the shape to select both the stroke and the fill. Select Modify > Group.

2. Click the fill area and move the shape around the left side of the Stage, as desired, to place it.

Create a logo with the Pen tool

The Pen tool offers a way to draw precise straight or curved line segments. You click to create points on straight line segments, and drag to create points on curved line segments. You can adjust the segments by adjusting points on the line. You'll use the Pen tool to create the logo.

1. In the Tools panel, select the Pen tool.

2. Click the dot next to the number 1, and then click the dot next to the number 2 to create a straight line segment.

3. Click the dot next to the number 3 and next to the number 4 in sequence (as though you were completing a dot-to-dot drawing). You create the straight line segments that comprise the logo.

4. To close the path, position the Pen tool over the first anchor point (the dot by number 1). A small circle appears next to the pen tip when it is positioned correctly. Click to close the path. After the path is closed, it fills with the selected fill color.

   By default, selected curve points appear as hollow circles, and selected corner points appear as hollow squares.

5. With the Selection tool, move the pointer around the logo that you created.

When you move the pointer over a corner point, which you can drag to create various angles, the pointer appears as follows:

When you move the pointer over a curved line segment (you don't have curve points in your logo), which you can drag to create various curved lines, the pointer appears as follows:

Summary

Congratulations on learning how to use some of the various drawing tools in Flash. In a few minutes, you learned how to accomplish the following tasks:

- Create a polygon.
- Rotate a shape.
- Cut out a shape within a shape.
- Transform artwork.
- Copy strokes.
- Draw lines with the Line tool.
- Select and add a fill color.
- Group a shape.
- Create a logo with the Pen tool.

To learn more about creating art in Flash, see "Drawing," in Flash Help.

CHAPTER 13

Creating Graphics: Create a Timeline Animation

13

Macromedia Flash Basic 8 and Macromedia Flash Professional 8 provide powerful tools for creating animation. Most simple animation in Flash is done using a process known as *tweening*. Tweening is short for "in between" and refers to filling in the frames between two keyframes so that a graphic displayed in the first keyframe changes into the graphic displayed in the second keyframe.

There are two types of tweening that you can create in Flash—a *motion tween* and a *shape tween*. The main difference between motion tweening and shape tweening is that motion tweening operates on grouped objects or symbols, and shape tweening is used with objects that are not symbols and are ungrouped.

You can print this tutorial by downloading a PDF version of it from the Macromedia Flash Documentation page at www.macromedia.com/go/fl_documentation.

In this tutorial, you will complete the following tasks:

Set up your workspace

First, you'll open the start file for the lesson and set up your workspace to use an optimal layout for taking lessons.

1. To open your start file, in Flash select File > Open and navigate to the file:

    -   In Windows, browse to *boot drive*\Program Files\Macromedia\ Flash 8\Samples and Tutorials\Tutorial Assets\ Creating Graphics\Timeline Animation and double-click animation_start.fla.

    -   On the Macintosh, browse to *Macintosh HD*/Applications/ Macromedia Flash 8/Samples and Tutorials/ Tutorial Assets/ Creating Graphics/Timeline Animation and double-click animation_start.fla.

> **NOTE** The Timeline Animation folder contains completed versions of lesson FLA files for your reference.

2. Select File > Save As and save the document with a new name, in the same folder, to preserve the original start file.

3. Select Window > Workspace Layout > Default to modify your workspace for taking lessons.

4. In the Stage View pop-up menu, in the upper-right side of the Timeline, select Show Frame to view both the Stage and the workspace.

5. If necessary, drag the lower edge of the Timeline (Window > Timeline) down to enlarge the Timeline view.

    You can also use the scroll bar to scroll through the layers.

Create a motion tween

You create a motion tween by defining properties for an instance, a grouped object, or text in a starting keyframe, and then changing the object's properties in a subsequent keyframe. Flash creates the animation from one keyframe to the next in the frames between the keyframes.

To create a motion tween, you'll take an instance of a tire symbol and make it appear to bounce.

1. In the Timeline (Window > Timeline), double-click the Layer 1 title and type **TireAnim.** Press Enter (Windows) or Return (Macintosh) to rename the layer.

2. With the TireAnim layer still selected, drag the Tire movie clip from the Library window (Window > Library) to the Stage, positioning it above the tire shadow.

3. Use the Selection tool to reposition the tire, if necessary.

4. With the Selection tool still selected, in the TireAnim layer, select Frame 30. Then press F6 to insert a keyframe.

5. Select Frame 15 and press F6 to add another keyframe.

6. With the playhead still on Frame 15, press Shift to move the tire in a straight line, and drag the tire up.

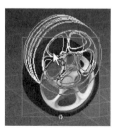

7. In the TireAnim layer, select any frame between Frames 2 and 14. In the Property inspector, select Motion from the Tween pop-up menu.

    An arrow appears in the Timeline between the two keyframes.

8. Select any frame between Frames 16 and 29. Again, use the Tween pop-up menu in the Property inspector to select Motion.

9. Select File > Save to save your changes.

Create a shape tween

With shape tweening, you specify attributes for a shape in one keyframe, and then modify the shape or draw another shape in a subsequent keyframe. As with motion tweening, Flash creates the animation in the frames between the keyframes.

You'll now set up a tween for the tire's shadow so that as the tire bounces, the shadow moves and fades.

1. Click the ShadowAnim layer to select it.

2. Select Frame 30 and press F6 to insert a keyframe; then select Frame 15 and press F6 to insert a keyframe.

3. With the playhead on Frame 15, select the Selection tool. Drag the tire shadow slightly up and to the right.

4. With Frame 15 still selected, select the Eyedropper tool in the Tools panel, and then click the shadow object.

5. If the Color Mixer is not already open, select Window > Color Mixer to open it, and change the Alpha value from 25% to 10%.

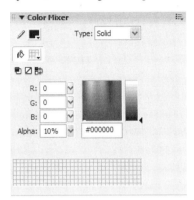

6. Click the pop-up menu control in the upper-right side of the Color Mixer and select Close Panel.

7. Select any frame between Frames 2 and 14 on the ShadowAnim layer. In the Property inspector, select Shape from the Tween pop-up menu.

8. On the ShadowAnim layer, select any frame between Frames 16 and 29. Again, use the Tween pop-up menu in the Property inspector to select Shape.

Copy and paste keyframes in an animation

For the tire to look realistic as it bounces, it should compress slightly on each bounce. You can create this effect by transforming the shape of the tire in Frame 1 of the animation, and copying that frame in Frame 30.

1. With the Selection tool, select Frame 1 of the TireAnim layer. Then press F6 to add a keyframe.

   A new keyframe is added and the playhead moves to Frame 2.

2. Select Frame 1 of the TireAnim layer again.

3. In the Tools panel, select the Free Transform tool.

The tire is selected, and transform handles appear around it.

4. Select the transformation center point (the small circle near the center of the movie clip) and drag it to the bottom of the tire.

The center point snaps to the lower-middle transform handle.

5. On the Stage, drag the upper-middle transform handle down to slightly compress the tire shape.

If necessary, drag the tire to align it over the shadow. To view the positioning, drag the playhead over Frames 1 and 2.

6. Save your file.

> **NOTE** Always save your document before attempting to manipulate tweens, including copying, cutting, and pasting frames. If you make an error, you can revert to your saved document.

7. Right-click (Windows) or Control-click (Macintosh) Frame 1 of the TireAnim layer and select Copy Frames from the context menu.

8. Select Frame 29 of the TireAnim layer and press F6 to insert a keyframe.

9. In Frame 30 of the TireAnim layer, right-click (Windows) or Control-click (Macintosh) and select Paste Frames from the context menu.

10. Select Control > Test Movie to view the animation.

11. Close the SWF file window to return to the authoring environment.

Change the speed of the animation

When you tested the animation, you might have noticed that the tire bounces rather slowly. You can change the speed of an animation by changing the number of frames that play per second, and by setting positive and negative easing values, which determine the rate of acceleration and deceleration.

Change the frames per second speed

The frame rate, measured in frames per second (fps) is the speed at which the animation plays. By default, Flash animations play at a rate of 12 fps, which is ideal for web animation. Sometimes, however, it's desirable to change the fps rate. You'll now change the frame rate to 36 frames per second, which will make the tire appear to bounce more rapidly.

1. Click the Stage, away from any objects.

2. In the Property inspector, type **36** in the Frame Rate text box.

   The frame rate applies to the entire Flash document, not just to an animation within the document.

Change the acceleration and deceleration

By default, tweened frames play at a constant speed. With easing, you can create a more realistic rate of acceleration and deceleration. Positive values begin the tween rapidly and decelerate the tween toward the end of the animation. Negative values begin the tween slowly and accelerate the tween toward the end of the animation. You'll now add both positive and negative easing values to your animation.

1. On the TireAnim layer, select any frame between Frames 2 and 14. Then in the Property inspector, in the Ease text box, type **100**. Press Enter (Windows) or Return (Macintosh).

2. On the same layer, select any frame between Frames 16 and 29. Then in the Ease text box, type **-100**. Press Enter or Return.

3. On the ShadowAnim layer, select any frame between Frames 2 and 14. Then in the Ease text box, type **100**. Press Enter or Return.

4. In the same layer, select any frame between Frames 16 and 29. Then in the Ease text box, type **-100**. Press Enter or Return.

Test the SWF file

You'll test your document to view the animation and see if it works as expected.

1. Save your document and select Control > Test Movie.

2. When you finish viewing the animation, close the SWF file window.

Summary

Congratulations on learning how to animate objects in Flash. In just a few minutes, you learned how to accomplish the following tasks:

- Create an animation using motion tweening.
- Create an animation using shape tweening.
- Copy and paste keyframes in an animation.
- Change the speed of an animation.

You can also use Timeline effects to quickly add animation effects to text, graphics, images, and symbols. For more information, see "Creating Motion," in Flash Help.

To learn more about Flash, take another lesson.

CHAPTER 14

Creating Graphics: Making Animations with Easing (Flash Professional only)

14

This tutorial guides you through the process of using the tweening tools in Macromedia Flash Basic 8 and Macromedia Flash Professional 8. *Tweening* is the process of animating a graphic by setting starting and ending values for its properties and letting Flash calculate the values in between. The term *tween* comes from "in between."

A simple example of a tween would be to place a graphic at the top of the Stage and then add several frames to the Timeline and move the graphic to the bottom of the Stage in the last frame. By letting Flash fill in the position values for the frames in between, you can easily create a smooth animation of the graphic from the top of the Stage to the bottom.

Flash Professional also lets you exercise fine control over how the tweened property values are calculated, so you can easily create more complex animations. By using the Custom Ease In / Ease Out window, you can control the speed at which the changes to properties are applied at the beginning, middle, and end of your animations. Careful use of this window can yield visually compelling results.

This tutorial takes you through the process of creating an animation by tweening different properties of a graphic using the various tweening controls in the Flash authoring environment.

After examining the completed animation, you'll begin by opening a starter Flash document and end by publishing the document for web playback. The tutorial should take approximately 20 minutes to complete.

Before you take this tutorial you should read "Flash Basics," in Flash Help.

In this tutorial, you will complete the following tasks:

The tweening tutorial workflow includes the following tasks:

- "Examine the completed FLA file" on page 163 allows you to look at the completed Flash file. In the process, you will become familiar with the construction of the animation example and what you will be building in this tutorial.

- "Open the starter document" on page 165 lets you begin the tutorial with a FLA file that has some graphics already created for you. You will apply animation effects to these graphics.

- "Create a motion tween" on page 165 shows you the steps needed to apply a typical motion tween.

- "Use easing controls" on page 168 shows you how to finely control how Flash calculates the motion of your animations.

- "Create a motion tween with an alpha setting" on page 174 shows you the steps needed to animate alpha transparency values.

Examine the completed FLA file

As you examine the finished version of the application you'll create, you will also look at the Flash workspace.

In subsequent sections, you'll go through the steps to create the application yourself.

Open the authoring document

It's helpful to analyze the completed authoring document, which is a FLA file, to see how the author designed the animation and understand what you are going to create.

The files for this tutorial are located in the Samples and Tutorials folder in the Flash application folder. For many users, particularly in educational settings, this folder is read-only. Before proceeding with the tutorial, you should copy the entire Animation Easing tutorial folder to the writable location of your choice.

On most computers, you will find the Animation Easing tutorial folder in the following locations:

- In Windows: *boot drive*\Program Files\Macromedia\Flash 8\
  Samples and Tutorials\Tutorial Assets\Creating Graphics\
  Animation Easing

- On the Macintosh: *boot drive*/Applications/Macromedia Flash 8/
  Samples and Tutorials/Tutorial Assets/Creating Graphics/
  Animation Easing

Copy the Animation Easing folder to another location on your hard disk that you have write access to. In the Animation Easing folder, you will find a Flash file called tween_finished.fla. Double-click the file to open it in Flash. You now see the completed tutorial file in the Flash authoring environment.

Review the completed FLA file

In the completed FLA file, you will see a graphic of an eight ball with a shadow beneath it on a green background. The illustration looks like this:

The completed FLA file

There are two tweens in the document:

- A motion tween of the ball bouncing down to the green surface.
- A motion tween of the shadow becoming larger and smaller according to the proximity of the eight ball.

There are two ways to see the animation in action.

See the animation play in a separate window as a SWF file

To see the animation play in a separate window as a SWF file, select Control > Test Movie.

See the animation on the Stage in the Flash authoring environment

To see the animation on the Stage in the Flash authoring environment, drag the red playhead across the Timeline.

Close the application

To close the document, select File > Close.

If you prefer to keep the finished file open as a reference while working with the starter file, be careful not to edit it or save any changes to it.

Open the starter document

Now that you have seen the completed file, it is time to create your own Flash document. To get started, you'll open a starter file that contains a few graphics to which you will apply animations.

In the Animation Easing folder, open the file called tween_start.fla. This file contains some graphics that you will use to create the animation.

Create a motion tween

To animate the eight-ball graphic over time, you need to insert enough frames in the Timeline to lengthen the time from the beginning of the FLA file to its end. In this section, you will add frames to the Timeline and then create a motion tween within those frames.

Add the necessary frames to the Timeline

To add the necessary frames to the Timeline:

1. In the Timeline, drag the pointer to select all the frames from 1 to 60 in all four layers.

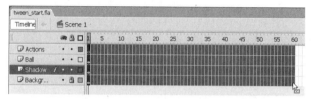

Selecting multiple frames in the Timeline

2. Select Insert > Timeline > Frame. You should see the frames added to all four layers in the Timeline.

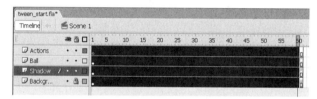

The frames added to the Timeline

Create a motion tween in the new frames

To create a motion tween in the new frames:

1. Select Frame 61 of the layer named Ball.

2. Select Insert > Timeline > Keyframe.

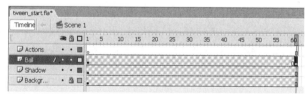

The keyframe added in Frame 61 of the Timeline

3. On the Stage, press Shift and drag the eight ball downward until the bottom of the eight ball is in the middle of the shadow graphic.

The eight ball correctly placed on the shadow

You have now defined a new position for the eight ball on the Stage in Frame 61. The ball now has one position for the first 60 frames, and a different position for the keyframe in Frame 61. When you define the motion tween, Flash calculates the positions in each frame for the eight ball, that is, between its original position above the Stage and its final position in the middle of the shadow.

4. In the Timeline, click the Ball layer name. This selects all the frames in that layer.

5. In the Property inspector, select Motion from the Tween menu. This applies the motion tween to the selected frames.

The Motion selected in the Tween menu of the Property inspector

6. In the Timeline, drag the playhead from Frame 1 to Frame 61. You will see the eight ball animate downward towards the shadow graphic.

> **NOTE** The speed of the ball's motion is constant throughout the animation. In the next section you will learn to control the speed with which your animations begin and end their motion.

7. Select File > Save As.

8. Name the file **my_tween_start.fla** and click OK.

Use easing controls

You can control the speed at which your animations start and stop with the easing controls in Flash. The term *easing* is used because when you make an animation, such as dropping the eight ball slowly and then speeding it up, it is considered to be "easing in" to its motion. When slowing an animation at the end, it is said to be "easing out." Flash also allows you to perform easing in the middle of a tween with its custom easing controls.

Ease in the eight-ball animation

1. In the Timeline, select the entire Ball layer by clicking the layer name.

2. In the Property inspector, drag the Ease slider down until the value is -100.

This will provide the maximum amount of easing in, thereby causing the eight-ball motion to start slowly and accelerate.

The Ease slider set to -100

3. Drag the playhead across the Timeline and observe the animation speed.

Ease out the eight-ball animation

1. In the Timeline, select the entire Ball layer by clicking the layer name.

2. In the Property inspector, drag the Ease slider up until the value is 100.

   This will provide the maximum amount of easing out, thereby causing the eight-ball motion to start abruptly and then decelerate.

3. Drag the playhead across the Timeline and observe the animation speed.

4. In the Timeline, select the entire Ball layer.

5. In the Property inspector, drag the Ease slider down until the value is 0.

   This will remove the easing from the animation.

Flash also provides more precise control of how easing occurs and allows you to add easing in the middle of a tween. In the next section, you will apply custom easing settings to the animation instead of using the Ease slider.

Add custom easing settings to the eight-ball tween

1. In the Timeline, select the entire Ball layer.

2. In the Property inspector, click Edit next to the Ease slider.

The Edit button in the Property inspector

The Custom Ease In / Ease Out dialog box displays a graph representing the degree of motion over time. Frames are represented by the horizontal axis, and the percentage of change is represented by the vertical axis.

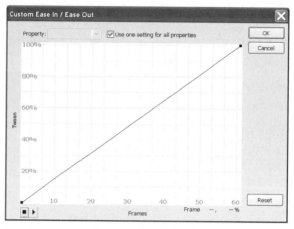

The Custom Ease In / Ease Out dialog box

3. In the Custom Ease In / Ease Out dialog box, Control-click (Windows) or Command-click (Macintosh) on the diagonal line where it crosses Frame 20 in the horizontal axis and on about 32% in the vertical axis. Click just once. This adds a new control point to the line.

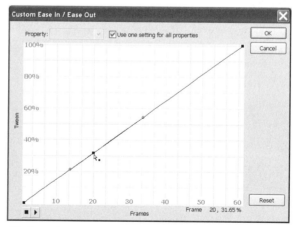

Clicking the Ease In / Ease Out diagonal line

4. Drag the line to the top of the graph (the 100% line) while keeping it at Frame 20 on the horizontal axis. The line is now a complex curve.

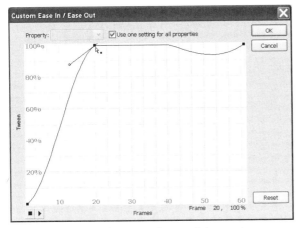

Dragging the control point to the top of the graph

5. Drag the left vertex handle of the new control point to the right until it touches the control point. Drag the right vertex handle to the left until it touches the control point. This makes the curve pass through the control point with a simple sharp angle.

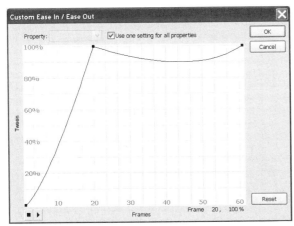

The control point with the vertex handles dragged onto the point

6. Control-click (Windows) or Command-click (Macintosh) the flat part of the curve at the top of the graph near Frame 32 and drag the new point downward to approximately 76% along the vertical axis.

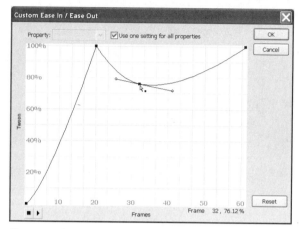

Dragging the point at Frame 32

7. Drag the vertex handles so that the line connecting them to the control point is horizontal and each handle is the same distance from the control point.

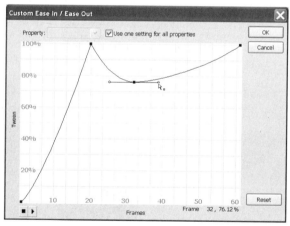

Dragging the vertex handles

8. Control-click (Windows) or Command-click (Macintosh) the curve at about Frame 44 and drag it up to the 100% line.

9. Drag the vertex handles for the new control point onto the control point.

10. Control-click (Windows) or Command-click (Macintosh) the curve at about Frame 52 and drag it down to about 95% on the vertical axis.

11. Drag the vertex handles so that the line connecting them to the control point is horizontal and each handle is the same distance from the control point.

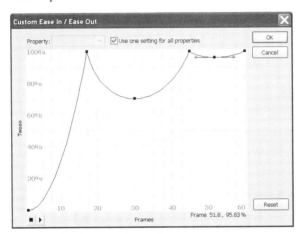

The completed Ease In / Ease Out curve

You have now created a complex easing curve that represents a bouncing eight ball instead of a simple one-way motion tween. You can use the Play button in the Custom Ease In / Ease Out dialog box to preview your animation on the Stage while you experiment with the tween curve.

12. In the lower-left corner of the Custom Ease In / Ease Out dialog box, click Play. Review the live preview of your animation on the Stage.

13. Click OK to close the dialog box.

14. Select File > Save to save your FLA file.

Create a motion tween with an alpha setting

In this section, you will create a tween of the alpha value of the shadow graphic that appears under the eight ball. Because the changes in the shadow should match the speed and timing of the bouncing eight ball, you will use the same easing curve you created in the previous section.

Create the tween of the alpha value for the shadow

1. In the Timeline, select Frame 61 of the layer called Shadow.
2. Select Insert > Timeline > Keyframe.
3. Drag the playhead to Frame 1.
4. Click outside the Stage to deselect all selections.
5. Click the shadow movie clip on the Stage.
6. In the Property inspector, select Alpha from the Color menu.
7. Drag the Alpha slider down until the value is 25%. You have now set the alpha value to 25% in Frame 1 and 100% in Frame 61.

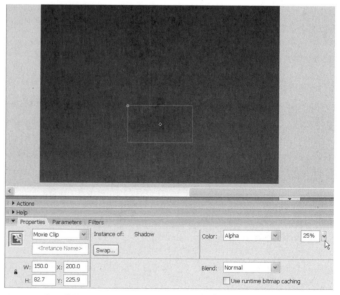

Setting the alpha value of the Shadow movie clip on the Stage to 25%

8. In the Timeline, click the layer named Ball to select the frames in that layer.

9. In the Property inspector, click Edit next to the Ease slider.

10. In the Custom Ease In / Ease Out dialog box, press Control-C (Windows) or Command-C (Macintosh) to copy the easing curve you applied to the ball tween.

11. Click Cancel to dismiss the dialog box.

12. In the Timeline, click the layer named Shadow to select all the frames in that layer.

13. In the Property inspector, select Motion from the Tween menu.

14. Click Edit next to the Ease slider.

15. In the Custom Ease In / Ease Out dialog box, press Control+V (Windows) or Command+V (Macintosh) to paste the easing curve from the ball tween.

16. Click Play in the dialog box to preview the animation on the Stage.

    By applying the same curve to the Shadow tween, you have made the transparency of the shadow animate according to the proximity of the ball. This way the shadow appears to become darker as the ball approaches the surface and lighter as the ball bounces away from the surface.

17. Click OK to close the dialog box.

18. Select File > Save to save your FLA file.

Test the application

At any point during authoring, you can test how your application plays as a SWF file. Because this tutorial contains no animation or interactivity, the file will look the same in test mode as it does in authoring mode.

1. Select File > Save to save your FLA file.

2. Select Control > Test Movie.

3. When you finish viewing the application, close the SWF file by clicking the close box in the test window.

You have now completed a successful complex animation using the custom easing controls in Flash. By using these controls while tweening the various properties of objects on the Stage, you can create a wide range of complex motions and interesting visual effects.

CHAPTER 15

Creating Graphics: Applying Gradients

15

This tutorial guides you through the process of using the gradient tools in Macromedia Flash Basic 8 and Macromedia Flash Professional 8. With Flash, you can create simple color gradients and complex gradient effects. In this tutorial, you learn how to do some of both.

A *gradient* is an area of a graphic where one color changes into another color. Flash can create two main types of gradients: linear and radial. Linear gradients change color along a single axis, such as horizontal or vertical. A radial gradient changes color in an outward direction starting from a focal point. You can adjust the direction of the gradient, its colors, the location of the focal point, and many other properties of gradients.

The following illustrations show the two types of gradients:

A two-color linear gradient from red to black

A two-color radial gradient from red to black

This tutorial takes you through the steps to create an illustration using an assortment of gradients.

After examining the completed illustration, you'll begin by opening a starter Flash document and end by publishing the document for web playback. The tutorial should take approximately 20 minutes to complete.

Before you take this tutorial you should read "Flash Basics," in Flash Help.

In this tutorial, you will complete the following tasks:

The tutorial in this chapter follows the order of a typical workflow for creating a Flash application. Other workflows are also possible.

The tutorial workflow includes the following tasks:

- "Examine the completed FLA file" on page 179 allows you to look at the completed Flash document.

- "Open the starter document" on page 181 lets you begin the tutorial with a FLA file that has some graphics already created for you. You will apply gradient effects to these graphics.

- "Apply a linear gradient" on page 181 shows you the steps needed to apply a linear gradient with specific colors.

- "Create a radial gradient" on page 183 shows you the steps needed to apply a radial gradient and make adjustments to its focal point.

- "Apply the finishing touches" on page 187 shows you the steps for performing a transform operation on a gradient. A transform operation is a change in an object's size or shape. You will also add a few more gradient effects to complete the illustration.

- "Test the application" on page 191 shows you how to publish your Flash document to a SWF file and view it in a web browser.

Examine the completed FLA file

As you examine the finished version of an application you'll create, you will also look at the Flash workspace.

In subsequent sections, you'll go through the steps to create the application yourself.

Open the authoring document

It's helpful to analyze the completed authoring document, which is a FLA file, to see how the author designed the illustration and understand what you are going to create.

The files for this tutorial are located in the Samples and Tutorials folder in the Flash application folder. For many users, particularly in educational settings, this folder is read-only. Before proceeding with the tutorial, you should copy the entire gradient tutorial folder to the writable location of your choice.

On most computers, you will find the Gradients tutorial folder in the following locations:

- In Windows: *boot drive*\Program Files\Macromedia\Flash 8\ Samples and Tutorials\Tutorial Assets\Creating Graphics\Gradients.

- On the Macintosh: *boot drive*/Applications/Macromedia Flash 8/ Samples and Tutorials/Tutorial Assets/Creating Graphics/Gradients.

Copy the Gradients folder to another location on your hard disk that you have write-access to. In the Gradients folder, you will find a Flash file called gradients_finished.fla. Double-click the file to open it in Flash. You now see the completed tutorial file in the Flash authoring environment.

Review the completed FLA file

In the completed FLA file, you will see the combined effects of several gradients. The illustration looks like this:

There are five gradients in the illustration:

- A gradient from black to green on the background.
- A gradient from black to green to black on the bottom of the eight ball.
- Another from white to black in the highlight on the top of the eight ball.
- A subtle gradient on the white circle surrounding the number "8."
- A radial gradient in the shadow beneath the eight ball.

Close the completed FLA file

To close the document, select File > Close.

If you prefer to keep the finished file open as a reference while working with the starter file, be careful not to edit it or save any changes to it.

Open the starter document

Now that you have seen the completed file, it is time to create your own Flash document. To get started, you'll open a starter file that contains a few graphics to which you will apply gradients.

1. In Flash, select File > Open.
2. Navigate to the following directory:
    - In Windows: *Hard Disk*\Program Files\Macromedia\ Flash 8\Samples and Tutorials\Tutorial Assets\Creating Graphics\
    - On the Macintosh: *Hard Disk*/Applications/Macromedia Flash 8/ Samples and Tutorials/Tutorial Assets/Creating Graphics/
3. Open the gradients_start.fla file.

Apply a linear gradient

In this section you will add a linear gradient to the background.

1. Click the Selection tool in the Tools panel.
2. Select the gray box in the layer named Background.
3. Select Window > Color Mixer to display the Color Mixer panel.
4. In the Color Mixer's Type pop-up menu, select Linear.

5. Double-click the right gradient color swatch and select the color green (#006600).

Selecting the right gradient color swatch in the Color Mixer

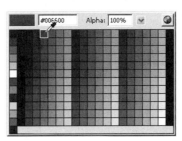

Selecting the color green #006600 in the Color Picker

6. Double-click the left gradient color swatch and select the color black (#000000).

7. Select the Gradient Transform tool from the Tools panel. The Gradient Transform controls appear on the Stage around the gradient.

The Gradient Transform tool

8. Drag the Gradient Rotate handle to rotate the linear gradient clockwise as shown.

The Gradient Rotate handle

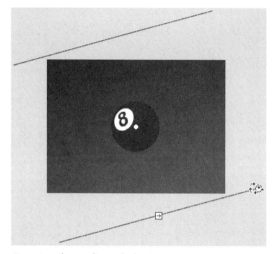

Rotating the gradient clockwise

9. Lock the Background layer in the Timeline to prevent further changes to this layer.

10. Select File > Save to save your FLA file.

Create a radial gradient

Next, you will add a radial gradient to the black eight ball.

1. Double-click the black circle in the layer called Ball. This opens the group containing the eight-ball shape.

2. Select the black circle shape. You will apply a gradient to this shape. Do not select the number "8" on the eight ball.

3. In the Color Mixer panel select Radial from the Type pop-up menu. Select Mirror Overflow mode from the Overflow pop-up menu.

The correct Radial Type and Mirror Overflow settings

4. Double-click the left gradient color swatch and select the color black (#000000).

5. Double-click the right gradient color swatch and type **002200** into the color text box. Press Enter.

6. Drag the left gradient color swatch to the right about three-fourths of the way as shown in the following illustration. This makes the green part of the gradient appear only in the outer 25% of the ball shape.

Dragging a gradient color swatch

7. Select the Zoom tool from the Tools panel and click the circle shape to magnify it.

8. Select the Gradient Transform tool in the Tools panel.

9. Rotate the radial gradient 90º clockwise by dragging the Gradient Rotate handle.

Dragging to rotate the gradient 90º clockwise.

10. Select the Focal Point control and drag it near the top of the circle.

Dragging the Focal Point control toward the top of the circle shape

11. Select the center control point and drag the entire gradient upward a short distance as shown in the following illustration. The mirrored overflow gradient is at the bottom of the circle.

Dragging the center control point upwards

12. Select the Selection tool in the Tools panel.

13. Double-click the Zoom tool to return the Stage area to a view of 100%.

14. Double-click the Stage area to deselect the eight-ball group.

15. Select File > Save to save your FLA file.

Create a transform gradient with a shape

In this section, you will create a gradient and then use the Free Transform tool to change its shape.

1. Select the Shadow layer in the Timeline.

2. Select the Oval tool in the Tools panel.

3. Hold down Shift and then drag on the Stage with the Oval tool to draw a circle approximately 150 pixels square. This should be about the same diameter as the eight ball.

4. In the Color Mixer's Type menu, select Radial.

5. Move the left gradient color swatch all the way to the left. You should have one swatch all the way to the left and one all the way to the right.

6. Double-click the left swatch and select the color black (#000000) in the Color Picker.

7. Double-click the right swatch to display the Color Picker.

8. Select the color black (#000000).

9. In the Color Picker, drag the Alpha slider down to zero. This creates a gradient from black to transparent, allowing the green background to show through the edge of the circle you just drew.

10. Select the Gradient Transform tool from the Tools panel and drag the Focal Point control of the gradient back to the center of the circle.

11. Select the Free Transform tool and scale the circle along the *y* (vertical) axis by dragging the top-center handle downward as shown in the following illustration.

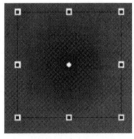

The gradient is transformed along with the shape transformation.

12. Select the Selection tool from the Tools panel.

13. Drag the shadow shape under the eight ball with the Selection tool.

14. Click outside the Stage to deselect the shadow.

15. Select File > Save to save your FLA file.

Apply the finishing touches

To complete the illustration, you will apply two more linear gradients: one to the white circle on the eight ball and one to make a highlight on the top of the eight ball.

Apply a gradient to the white circle on the eight ball

Next you will add a gradient to the white circle on the eight ball graphic.

1. Select the Selection tool from the Tools panel.

2. Double-click the eight ball group to edit the group.

3. Double-click the white circle group.

4. Select the white circle shape.

5. In the Color Mixer panel, assign the white circle shape a linear gradient by selecting Linear from the Type menu.

6. Select Nonrepeating from the Overflow menu.

7. Drag the left gradient color swatch all the way to the left and double-click it.

8. Select the color white (#FFFFFF) from the Color Picker.

9. Set the Alpha value for the white color swatch to 100%.

10. Drag the right color swatch all the way to the right and double-click it.

11. Select the color black (#000000) from the Color Picker.

12. Set the Alpha value for the black color swatch to 100%.

Your gradient settings should match those in the following illustration:

The Color Mixer with the correct settings for the gradient on the white circle

13. Select the Gradient Transform tool from the Tools panel.

14. Drag the Gradient Rotate handle approximately 120° clockwise.

The gradient rotated 120°

15. Select the Selection tool in the Tools panel.

16. Double-click the Stage twice to exit the white circle group and the eight-ball group.

17. Select File > Save to save your FLA file.

Apply a linear gradient to the highlight

In this section you will apply a linear gradient.

1. Click the red X icon in the layer named Highlight to reveal the shape in that layer. The shape appears at the top of the eight ball.

2. With the Selection tool, double-click the highlight shape to edit its group.

3. Select the highlight shape.

4. In the Color Mixer, select Linear from the Type menu.

5. Select Non-repeating from the Overflow menu.

6. Drag the left gradient color swatch all the way to the left and double-click it.

7. Select the color white (#FFFFFF) from the Color Picker.

8. Set the Alpha value for the left swatch to 0%.

9. Drag the right gradient color swatch all the way to the right and double-click it.

10. Select the color white from the Color Picker.

11. Set the Alpha value for the right swatch to 75%.

    Your gradient settings should match those in the following illustration:

The Color Mixer with the correct settings for the gradient on the highlight shape

12. With the highlight shape still selected, select the Gradient Transform tool from the Tools panel.

13. Drag the Gradient Rotate control 90º counterclockwise.

14. Drag the Gradient Scale control downward until it touches the top of the highlight shape.

The Gradient Scale control

Dragging the Gradient Scale control downward to touch the highlight shape

15. Select the Selection tool from the Tools panel.

16. Double-click outside the Stage twice to deselect the highlight group.

The finished Flash illustration looks like this:

17. Select File > Save to save your FLA file.

Test the application

At any point during authoring, you can test how your application plays as a SWF file. Because this tutorial contains no animation or interactivity, the file will look the same in test mode as it does in authoring mode.

1. Select File > Save to save your FLA file.

2. Select Control > Test Movie.

3. When you finish viewing the application, close the SWF file by clicking the close box in the test window.

You have now successfully applied a variety of gradients in Flash and created an attractive and realistic-looking illustration. By using the gradient tools in Flash, you can create an infinite range of visually interesting graphics and effects.

Creating Graphics: Apply Graphic Filters and Blends (Flash Professional Only)

16

This tutorial guides you through the process of creating eye-catching graphic effects using some of the authoring features in Macromedia Flash Professional 8 (Filters are not available in Flash Basic). By using the graphic filters and blend modes available in Flash, you can transform ordinary graphic objects into much more visually compelling content.

A graphic filter is a method that processes the pixels of a graphic object to produce a specific effect. For example, you can apply a blur filter to an object to make its edges appear softer, or you can apply a drop shadow filter to an object to make it appear with a shadow behind it.

A blend mode is a method of making the colors of a graphic object interact with the colors of other graphic objects beneath it. For example, by using the Lighten blend mode, you can make the parts of an object appear lighter in color to varying degrees depending on the colors of the objects beneath it.

If you have not already done so, Macromedia recommends that before you take this tutorial you read "Flash Basics," in Flash Help.

You can print this tutorial by downloading a PDF version of it from the Macromedia Flash Documentation page at www.macromedia.com/go/ fl_documentation.

In this tutorial, you will complete the following tasks:

Review your task

In this tutorial, you will add some graphics to the Stage and apply filters to them to create a realistic-looking image of a pool table with a narrow depth of field. The balls in the foreground and background will appear out of focus, as if seen through a camera.

The completed FLA file

To see the completed FLA file (Filters&Blends_finished.fla), browse to one of the following locations:

- In Windows: *Hard Disk*\Program Files\Macromedia\Flash 8\ Samples and Tutorials\Tutorial Assets\Creating Graphics\ Filters and Blends

- On the Macintosh: *Hard Disk*/Applications/Macromedia Flash 8/ Samples and Tutorials/Tutorial Assets/Creating Graphics/ Filters and Blends

Open the starter document

Now that you have seen the document you will create, it is time to create your own version of the document. The first thing to do is open the starter document, which contains the graphic objects you will use with the filter and blend features of Flash.

1. In Flash, select File > Open.

2. Browse to one of the following locations:

   ▪ In Windows: *Hard Disk*\Program Files\Macromedia\ Flash 8\Samples and Tutorials\Tutorial Assets\ Creating Graphics\Filters and Blends

   ▪ On the Macintosh: *Hard Disk*/Applications/Macromedia Flash 8/ Samples and Tutorials/Tutorial Assets/Creating Graphics/ Filters and Blends

3. Select the file named Filters&Blends_start.fla and click Open.

NOTE As you complete the tutorial, remember to save your work frequently.

Apply filters and blends

In the following sections, you will apply blends and filters to the 9ball and CueBall movie clips found in the Library panel.

Apply a blend to the 9ball movie clip

The first task you must perform in the starter file is to apply a blend effect to an instance of the 9ball outlines movie clip to make its colors combine with the colors of the 9ball movie clip. This achieves a realistic shiny pool ball look.

1. Open the Library panel (Window > Library).

2. Drag the 9ball movie clip from the Library panel to the lower-right corner of the Stage.

   This creates an new instance of the 9ball movie clip on the Stage.

3. Double-click the new 9ball instance to enter symbol-editing mode.

4. Drag the 9ball outlines movie clip from the Library panel onto the Stage so that it perfectly covers the 9ball instance.

   You can use the Arrow keys to make fine adjustments to the placement of the 9ball outlines instance.

5. With the 9ball outlines instance still selected, go to the Property inspector and select Multiply from the Blend menu.

6. Double-click outside the Stage to exit symbol-editing mode.

   The 9ball instance should still be selected on the Stage.

7. Open the Transform panel (Window > Transform).

8. In the Transform panel, click the Constrain check box.

9. Double-click the Width text box and enter **140**.

10. This makes the 9ball instance appear larger than the 8ball instance on the Stage.

11. Reposition the 9ball instance so it slightly overlaps the right edge of the 8ball instance on the Stage.

Apply a filter

The next step is to apply a blur filter to the 9ball movie clip to make it appear out of focus, as if it is in the foreground of the Stage.

1. With the 9ball instance still selected, click the Filters tab in the Property inspector.

2. In the Filters tab, click Add Filter and select Blur from the pop-up menu.

3. Drag the BlurX slider until the BlurX and BlurY value is 19.

   The BlurX and BlurY values are constrained to each other by default. Click the lock icon if they are not.

4. Click the Properties tab of the Property inspector.

5. In the Property inspector, enter the following values in the W, H, X, and Y text boxes:

   W: **210**
   H: **235**
   X: **315**
   Y: **155**

6. Click outside the Stage to deselect the 9ball instance.

Apply filters and blends to the cue ball

The last step is to use a color effect and a filter to make the cue ball appear to be in the background of the Stage.

1. Drag the CueBall movie clip from the Library panel to the upper-left corner of the Stage.

2. With the new CueBall instance still selected on the Stage, go to the Transform panel and enter **70** in the W (Width) and H (Height) text boxes.

    This makes the CueBall instance appear smaller than the 8ball instance.

3. With the CueBall instance still selected on the Stage, go to the Property inspector and select Brightness from the Color menu.

    A Brightness Amount slider appears to the right of the Color menu.

4. Drag the Brightness Amount slider until the value is -48%.

5. Enter the following values in the W, H, X, and Y text boxes:

    W: **105**

    H: **115**

    X: **95**

    Y: **105**

6. With the CueBall instance still selected on the Stage, click the Filters tab in the Property inspector.

7. Click Add Filter and select Blur from the Filter pop-up menu.

8. Drag the BlurX slider until the BlurX and BlurY values are each 13.

    These text boxes are constrained to match each other by default. Click the lock icon if they are not.

9. Click outside the Stage to deselect the CueBall instance.

You have now applied the graphic effects to create a realistic look of depth.

For more information about using filters and blends, see "Using Filters and Blends (Flash Professional only)," in Flash Help.

CHAPTER 17

Text: Add Text to a Document

Macromedia Flash Basic 8 and Macromedia Flash Professional 8 provide a variety of text features and options. This lesson introduces you to the three primary types of text you can add to a document. You can add *static text* for titles, labels, or other text content you want to appear in a document. You can also use *input text* options to allow viewers to interact with your Flash application—for example, to enter their name or other information in a form. The third type of text is *dynamic text*. You use dynamic text fields to display text that changes based on criteria you specify. For example, you might use a dynamic text field to add values stored in other text fields, such as the sum of two numbers. This tutorial shows you how to add text and text fields to a Flash document.

After taking this lesson, be sure to explore additional text options described in "Working with Text" in Flash Help.

You can print this tutorial by downloading a PDF version of it from the Macromedia Flash Documentation page at www.macromedia.com/go/fl_documentation.

In this tutorial, you will complete the following tasks:

Set up your workspace

First, you'll open the start file for the lesson and set up your workspace to use an optimal layout for taking lessons.

1. To open your start file, in Flash select File > Open and navigate to the file:

    - In Windows, browse to *boot drive*\Program Files\ Macromedia\Flash 8\Samples and Tutorials\Tutorial Assets\ Text\Add Text to a Document and double-click text_start.fla.

    - On the Macintosh, browse to *Macintosh HD*/Applications/ Macromedia Flash 8/Samples and Tutorials/Tutorial Assets/Text/ Add Text to a Document and double-click text_start.fla.

> **NOTE** The Add Text to a Document folder contains completed versions of the tutorial FLA files for your reference.

2. Select File > Save As and save the document with a new name, in the same folder, to preserve the original start file and to preserve the file's link to dependent files.

3. Select Window > Workspace Layout > Default to modify your workspace for taking lessons.

4. In the Stage View pop-up menu, in the upper-right side of the Timeline, select Show Frame to view both the Stage and the workspace.

5. In the Tools panel, click the Selection tool. Then in the Timeline, click the Static Text layer to select the layer you'll work in.

Create an expanding-width text block

You can define the size of a text block, or you can use a text block that expands to fit the text you write. You'll begin this lesson by simply adding text to a document.

1. Click in a blank area in the workspace to make sure no Timeline frames or objects on the Stage are selected.

2. In the Tools panel, select the Text tool.

3. In the text Property inspector, set the following options:

   - In the Text Type pop-up menu, select Static text, if it isn't already selected.

   - For Font, select Arial.

   - For Font Size, enter **13**.

   - Click the text color box and select the gray with a hexadecimal value of #666666.

   - Select Align Left, if it isn't already selected.

4. In the Timeline, select the Static Text layer.

5. With the Text tool still selected, click the Stage along the left edge of Text 1 guide, and type **Trio ZX2004 Safety Features**.

   By typing with the Text tool selected, you create a one-line text block that expands as you type. An expanding-width one-line static text block has a round handle in the upper-right corner.

   Trio ZX2004 Safety Features
   Text 1

6. If necessary, align the text above the Text 1 guide by clicking the Selection tool in the Tools panel and dragging the text that you typed to the guide.

> **NOTE**
> The Text 1 guide is on a guide layer, which doesn't appear in your SWF file.

Create a fixed-width text block

In addition to creating a line of text that expands as you type, you can create a text block that has a fixed width. Text that you enter into a fixed-width text block wraps to the next line at the edge of the block.

You'll now create a static text block with fixed dimensions.

1. Verify that the Static Text layer is still selected in the Timeline, and use the Selection tool to deselect any objects on the Stage or Timeline frames (click in the workspace, away from objects)

2. In the Tools panel, select the Text tool.

3. In the Property inspector, change the text size to 10 points.

4. On the Stage, drag your pointer over the area of the Text 2 guide.

   An extendable one-line static text block has a round handle in the upper-right corner, and a fixed-width static text block has a square handle.

5. Inside the text block that you created, type **Want to learn more?**

<table>
<tr><td>NOTE</td><td>You can drag the square handle for a text block to change its width. Additionally, you can double-click a square handle to convert it into a round expanding handle.</td></tr>
</table>

6. If necessary, align the text by clicking the Selection tool in the Tools panel and dragging the text that you typed above the Text 2 guide.

Edit text and change font attributes

When you select text, the Property inspector displays standard type formatting features. You can use the Property inspector to change font and size properties for a selected text object.

1. In the Tools panel, click the Selection tool. Double-click the text on the Stage that reads "Submit your contact information."

2. Select the letter S then type **Please s**, so that the text now reads "Please submit your contact information."

3. In the Tools panel, click the Selection tool. Use the Property inspector to select the bold style.

4. Click the text Fill Color control and select a different text color, such as another shade of gray.

Select device fonts

When you use a font installed on your system in a Flash document, Flash embeds the font information in the Flash SWF file to ensure that the font is displayed properly. In addition to embedding fonts, you can use the device fonts option. This option finds the fonts on a viewer's computer that most closely resemble the specified device font. You can use device fonts only with static text.

You'll specify that the selected text uses device fonts.

1. With the "Please submit your contact information" text still selected on the Stage, in the Font pop-up menu in the Property inspector, select _sans.

2. In the Property inspector, select Use Device Fonts.

   You will not see a difference in the text if you have the Arial font installed on your computer.

Add an input text field

You can use an input text field to allow viewers an opportunity to interact with your Flash application. For example, input text fields offer an easy way to create forms.

In a later lesson (select Help > Flash Tutorials > ActionScript: Create a Form with Conditional Logic and Send Data), you'll learn how to use an input text field to send data from Flash to a server. Now, you'll add a text field where viewers will enter their first name.

1. In the Timeline, select the Input Text layer.

2. Use the Selection tool to click in the workspace, away from the objects on the Stage.

3. In the Tools panel, select the Text tool.

4. In the text Property inspector, set the following options:

- Select Input Text in the Text Type pop-up menu
- Select Arial in the Font pop-up menu.
- For the font size, enter **8**.
- Click the text color box and select a shade of dark blue.

- Select the Alias Text button.

   The Alias Text button renders text so that it appears more readable at small sizes. For input text, this option is supported if the end user has Macromedia Flash Player 7 or later.

- Select Single Line in the Line Type pop-up menu, and verify that Show Border Around Text is selected.

   Single Line displays the text as one line. Show Border Around Text indicates the boundaries of the text field with a visible border.

5. On the Stage, drag the pointer in the area to the right of the First Name text to create an input text field.

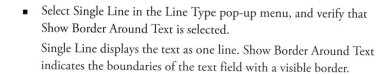

6. If necessary, use the Selection tool to reposition the input text field.

Copy a text field

One way to quickly duplicate an object on the Stage is to press Alt while dragging the object. The original object remains in place, allowing you to drag the duplicate. You'll press Alt to create two copies of the input text field that you created.

1. On the Stage, with the Selection tool selected, click the input text field that you created and press Alt. Drag a copy of the text field to the right of Last Name.

2. Alt-click the input text field that you just dragged, and then drag the new copy of the field to eMail Address.

Assign instance names to text fields

An input text field on the Stage is an instance of the ActionScript TextField object, to which you can apply properties and methods. As a best practice, you should name text field instances so that you or others working on the project can refer to the instance in ActionScript.

1. Select the input text field that you placed next to First Name. In the Property inspector, enter **firstName_txt** in the Instance Name text box.

2. Select the input text field that you placed next to Last Name. In the Property inspector, enter **lastName_txt** in the Instance Name text box.

3. Select the input text field that you placed next to eMail Address. In the Property inspector, enter **eMail_txt** in the Instance Name text box.

To learn more about the TextField object, see "Working with Text" in Flash Help.

Create a dynamic text field

Dynamic text can display text from external sources at runtime. Next, you'll create a dynamic text field that links to an external text file. The external text file you'll use is named safetyFeatures.txt. It is in the same folder as the lesson FLA file. The FLA file already contains ActionScript that displays the text when you test or publish the document.

1. In the Timeline, select the Dynamic Text layer. Use the Selection tool to click in the workspace, and to deselect any objects.

2. Select the Text tool in the Tools panel.

3. In the text Property inspector, set the following options:

   - Select Dynamic Text from the Text Type pop-up menu.
   - For Text Attributes, set Verdana as the text type, with a font size of **6**.
   - For Line Type, select Multiline to ensure the text wraps correctly.
   - Click the text color box and select a dark shade of gray.
   - Select Align Left as a paragraph attribute, if it isn't already selected.

4. On the Stage, drag to create a text field in the area between the two horizontal rules.

Trio ZX2004 Safety Features
Text 1

5. In the Instance Name text box of the Property inspector, name the dynamic text field **newFeatures_txt**.

The ActionScript in this document loads an external text file, which is in the same folder as your document. The ActionScript is set up to load the text into a field named newFeatures_txt.

Specify format options

The Format Options dialog box allows you to specify margin and indentation settings for the text.

1. With the dynamic text field still selected on the Stage, click Format in the Property inspector.

2. In the Left Margin text box, enter 5, and in the Right Margin text box, enter 5. Then click OK.

The dynamic text now has 5-pixel left and right margins within the text field.

View ActionScript for the dynamic text field

You can view the ActionScript that loads text from the external text file into the dynamic text field. This script uses LoadVars actions to load the safetyfeatures.txt content in the newFeatures text field.

1. In the Timeline, select Frame 1 of the Actions layer.

2. Select Window > Actions, or press F9.

    The ActionScript appears as follows:

```
// Load text as variable and assign it to the
// dynamic text field
var features_lv:LoadVars = new LoadVars();
features_lv.onLoad = onText;
features_lv.load("safetyfeatures.txt");
function onText(success:Boolean) {
  if (success) {
    newFeatures_txt.text = features_lv.safetyfeatures;
  } else {
    newFeatures_txt.text = "unable to load text file.";
  }
}
```

3. Close the Actions panel.

Test the SWF file

Save and test the document to ensure that the dynamic text loads correctly.

1. Select File > Save; then select Control > Test Movie.

    In the SWF file window, text from the external text file should appear in the dynamic text field that you created. (If the text does not appear as expected, check that you entered the instance name correctly: newFeatures_txt. Also check that you saved your copy of the practice file in the same folder as the original text_start file.)

2. Type in the input text fields.

3. When you finish testing the file, close the SWF file window.

Check spelling

Flash Basic 8 and Flash Professional 8 introduce new features that let you check spelling in most places where text occurs in your document, including text fields, layer names, and ActionScript strings. To check spelling, you first configure the Spelling Setup options, and then run the spell checker.

1. Select Text > Spelling Setup.

2. Verify that Check Text Fields Content is selected, and that you've selected the appropriate dictionary. Select any other options, as desired. Then click OK.

3. Select Text > Check Spelling and respond to the dialog boxes that the spell checker presents. When you finish checking spelling, save your document.

Summary

Congratulations on learning the basic ways in which to add text to your document. In a few minutes, you learned how to accomplish the following tasks:

- Create an expanding-width text block.
- Create a fixed-width text block.
- Edit text and change font attributes.
- Select device fonts.
- Add an input text field.
- Copy a text field.
- Assign instance names to text fields.
- Create a dynamic text field.
- View ActionScript that links the text field to an external text file.
- Set up and check spelling.

To learn more about the great variety of options you have when adding text to your document, see "Working with Text," in Flash Help.

CHAPTER 18

ActionScript: Use Script Assist mode

18

This tutorial guides you through using Script Assist mode in Macromedia Flash Basic 8 and Macromedia Flash Professional 8.

Script Assist mode prompts you to enter the elements of a script, and helps you to add simple interactivity to your SWF file (a compressed version of a Flash .fla file with the .swf extension) or application more easily. Script Assist mode is ideal for users who either aren't comfortable writing their own scripts, or who just appreciate the ease of use the tool provides.

Used in conjunction with the Actions panel, Script Assist mode prompts you to select options and enter parameters. For example, instead of writing your own script, you can select a language element from the Actions toolbox (or the Add (+) command on the toolbar), drag it onto the Script pane, and then use Script Assist mode to help you complete the script.

This tutorial guides you through the steps of using Script Assist mode to add interactivity to a Flash application. You will add ActionScript code to an object (a button) and to frames in the Timeline. This tutorial also demonstrates some best practices for adding scripts to your Flash document.

After examining the completed Flash application, you'll begin by opening a starter Flash document and end by testing the interactivity you've added to an application by using Script Assist mode. The tutorial should take approximately 20 minutes to complete.

Before you take this tutorial, read "Flash Basics" in Flash Help.

In this tutorial, you will complete the following tasks:

The tutorial in this chapter follows the order of a typical workflow for creating a Flash application. Other workflows are also possible.

The tutorial workflow includes the following tasks:

- "Examine the completed FLA file" on page 211 allows you to look at the completed Flash document.

- "Open the starter document" on page 213 lets you begin the tutorial with a FLA file (a Flash file with the .fla extension) that has the elements to which you'll use Script Assist mode to add ActionScript.

- "Add a script to a button by using Script Assist mode" on page 213 shows you how to use Script Assist mode to add a script directly to a button object on the Stage.

- "Add frame scripts to the Timeline by using Script Assist mode" on page 218 shows you how to use Script Assist mode to place scripts on a frame in the Timeline that affect buttons on the Stage. Placing code in a frame on the Timeline instead of placing code directly on objects on the Stage is a better approach to organizing ActionScript within your Flash applications.

- "Add a frame script to the Title movie clip" on page 221 shows you how to place code in the final frame of a movie clip.

- "Test the application" on page 223 shows you how to publish your Flash document to a SWF file and view it in a web browser.

Examine the completed FLA file

As you examine the finished version of an application that you'll create, you'll also look at the Flash workspace.

In subsequent sections you'll go through the steps to create the application yourself.

Open the authoring document

It's helpful to analyze the completed authoring document, which is a FLA file, to see how the author designed the application. You should examine what kinds of scripts were used to add interactivity, and understand what you are going to create.

The files for this tutorial are located in the Samples and Tutorials folder in the Flash installation folder. For many users, particularly in educational settings, this folder is read-only. Before proceeding with the tutorial, copy the entire Script Assist tutorial folder to the writable location of your choice.

On most computers, you will find the Script Assist tutorial folder in the following locations:

■ In Windows: *boot drive*\Program Files\Macromedia\Flash 8\ Samples and Tutorials\Tutorial Assets\ActionScript\Script Assist.

■ On the Macintosh: *Macintosh HD*/Applications/Macromedia Flash 8/ Samples and Tutorials/Tutorial Assets/ActionScript/Script Assist.

Copy the Script Assist folder to another location on your hard disk to which you have access. In the Script Assist folder, you will find a Flash file called scriptassist_complete.fla. Double-click the file to open it in Flash. You now see the completed tutorial file in the Flash authoring environment.

Review the completed FLA file

In the completed FLA file, you will see all the objects (buttons, movie clips, and graphics) that make up the sample application. The application, a Flash-based company information website, looks like this:

The completed FLA file

There are three movie clips in the application:

■ The Title movie clip, which displays the section titles of the site when the user clicks the corresponding navigation links (Home, About, Products, Contact).

■ The Menu and Menu tween movie clips, which display the primary navigation links (buttons) and together create an animation when the application is run.

The application has four buttons:

■ The About, Products, Contact, and Home buttons provide the navigation for the application.

In this tutorial you will add the ActionScript code to enable the buttons to navigate to the separate sections of the site.

Close the completed FLA file

To close the document, select File > Close.

If you prefer to keep the finished file open as a reference while working with the starter file, be careful not to edit it or save any changes to it.

Open the starter document

Now that you have seen the completed file, it is time to create your own Flash document. To get started, you'll open a starter file that contains the elements to which you will add ActionScript code using Script Assist mode.

To open the starter document:

1. In Flash, select File > Open.

2. Navigate to the following directory:

   - In Windows: *Hard Disk*\Program Files\ Macromedia\Flash 8\ Samples and Tutorials\Tutorial Assets\ActionScript\Script Assist.

   - On the Macintosh: *Macintosh HD*/Applications/ Macromedia Flash 8/Samples and Tutorials/Tutorial Assets/ ActionScript/Script Assist.

3. Open the scriptassist_start.fla file.

Add a script to a button by using Script Assist mode

In this section you'll use Script Assist mode to add a script to the Home button. When the sample application is run and the Home button is clicked, the Home title appears in the Title movie clip.

> **NOTE** This section demonstrates how you add scripts directly to objects. Although this approach can be convenient for adding interactivity to your Flash applications, you should follow best coding practices and add code to the Timeline rather than to individual objects. For more information, see "Add frame scripts to the Timeline by using Script Assist mode" on page 218.

1. Click the Selection tool in the Tools panel.

2. On the Timeline, select the "menu and button" layer.

   If the layer is locked, unlock it.

3. In the upper-right corner of the Stage, select the Home button.

4. In the Actions panel, you'll see the Script Assist button above the ActionScript editor.

Click Script Assist to display Script Assist mode.

With no functions selected, the Script Assist pane is blank.

Initially, the Script Assist portion of the Actions panel is blank. Script Assist mode prompts you to select options and set parameters for the functions that you add to the selected button. The parameters are displayed when you add an ActionScript function.

> **NOTE** You may notice that when Script Assist mode is enabled, you cannot directly edit code in the ActionScript editor, because it is read-only. All interaction with the code in the editor is through Script Assist mode with one important exception: you can highlight functions in the ActionScript editor and delete them.

5. To add a function to the button, click Add on the toolbar.

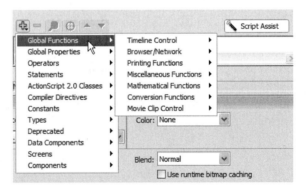

Clicking the Add button displays all of the predefined ActionScript functions.

6. From the Movie Clip Control option, select the on event handler.

An alternative method of adding ActionScript functions is to browse for and then select them from the Actions toolbox. The Add button on the Actions panel toolbar and the Actions toolbox display the same categories of functions and you can add functions to the editor from both.

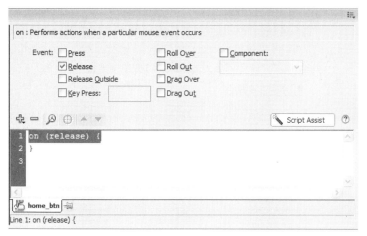

Script Assist mode prompts you to set the function's parameters.

The release event of the on event handler is selected by default.

You'll use the release event to trigger the script action when the user clicks Home.

7. Click Add again and then select the `goto()` function from the Global Functions > Timeline Control option.

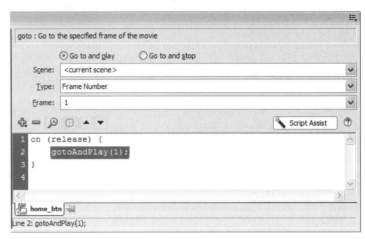

Adding the function that is triggered when the event occurs

The `goto()` function is added as the action of the `on` event handler. In other words, when the Home button is pressed (the `on` handler) and released (the `release` event), the `goto()` action is executed.

When the Home button is clicked, the movie clip should move to and stop at the Home frame of the Timeline. To do this, you use Script Assist mode to modify the default parameters of the `goto()` function.

8. In the Script Assist panel, select the Go To and Stop option.

9. Set the Type to Frame Label by selecting it from the Type pop-up menu.

10. In the Frame text box, enter **home**.

Modifying function parameters to complete the script

The changes you made with Script Assist mode are displayed in the ActionScript editor. You've just created a script without manually writing code in the ActionScript editor.

When you test the application, clicking the Home button will display the title "Home" in the Title movie clip, indicating that the Home frame is currently displayed.

Clicking the Home button displays "Home" in the Title movie clip.

You could repeat this process for the About, Products, and Contacts buttons. However, for these buttons you'll use an alternative and preferred method for creating scripts.

In each case, you want to display the related frames on the Timeline when each of the buttons are clicked; therefore, you will set the frame target of the gotoAndStop() function to the About, Products, and Contacts frames, as you've just done for the Home button.

Add frame scripts to the Timeline by using Script Assist mode

Rather than adding scripts to individual objects, and acting on objects directly but also dispersing code in many different places in your Flash document, place the scripts in a frame in the timeline instead. This section demonstrates how you add scripts to a timeline.

1. On the main Timeline, select Frame 1 of the Actions layer.

2. In the Actions panel toolbar, click Script Assist to display the Script Assist window.

3. From the Actions toolbox, select ActionScript 2.0 Classes > Movie > Button > Events and locate the on(release) event handler.

   Double-click the on(release) event handler to insert it into the ActionScript editor.

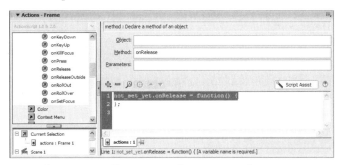

Using the Actions toolbox to insert functions into the script

You'll notice that code placed on a timeline behaves differently than code placed on objects. In the previous example, you had to specify the target object for the on(release) event handler. This is because you're not adding the script directly to the object, but rather, you're referring to it from the code in the timeline. It also explicitly uses the function keyword to declare a function. You'll see how to use Script Assist mode to handle these in the following steps.

4. Click in the Object text box.

   On the Actions panel toolbox, the Insert a Target Path button is enabled.

5. Click the Insert a Target Path button to display the Insert Target Path dialog box.

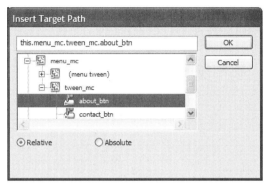

Selecting the target object from the Insert Target Path dialog box

6. Select the About button (`about_btn`) from the tween_mc movie clip.

7. Make sure that the Relative Path option is selected and then click OK. The target object (the Menu tween) is added.

The path to the target object is added to the event handler.

You now need to add the goto() function, the action that occurs when the About button is clicked.

1. Using the Actions toolbox or the Add button on the Actions panel toolbox, select Global Functions > Timeline Control and insert the goto function.

2. In the Script Assist pane, select the Go To and Stop option.

3. Set the Type to Frame Label by selecting it from the Type pop-up menu.

4. In the Frame text box, enter **about**.

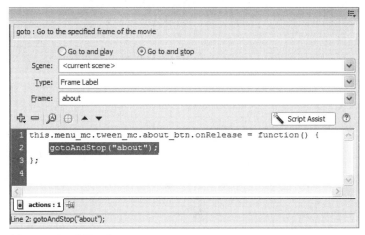

The completed Timeline script

Repeat this process for the Products and Contacts buttons. In each case, when the buttons are clicked, you want to display the related frames on the Timeline; therefore, set the frame target of the gotoAndStop() function to the Products and Contacts frames as you did for the About button.

Add a frame script to the Title movie clip

The final step is to add a script to the last frame of the Title movie clip. This script is used to display the text "Home" in the Title movie clip when its animation has completed.

1. From the Library panel, select the Title movie clip and its timeline is displayed.

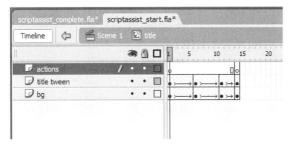

Selecting the Title movie clip timeline to add a script to the last frame

2. With the Actions layer selected, select the last frame (14) on the Timeline.

3. In the Actions panel, click Script Assist to display Script Assist mode.

4. Using either the Actions toolbox or the Add button on the Actions panel toolbar, select Global Functions > Timeline Control and insert the stop() function.

5. Next, using either the Actions toolbox or the Add button, select ActionScript 2.0 Classes > Movie > MovieClip > Methods > gotoAndStop.

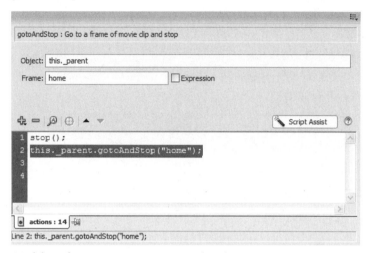

Modifying function parameters to complete the script

6. In the Script Assist panel, select the `gotoAndStop` action on line 2.
7. Click in the Object text box.
8. Click the Insert Target Path button.
9. In the Insert Target Path dialog box, click the `_root` object and click OK.
10. In the Frame text box, enter **home**.
11. Deselect the Expression checkbox.

   Now, when the `Title` movie clip reaches the last frame and the animation is complete, "Home" is displayed. This is the initial state of the application, after it loads and before the user clicks any of the buttons.

12. Save your work.

All of the scripts needed to run the sample application are now complete and the application is ready to be tested.

Test the application

At any point during authoring, you can test how your application plays as a SWF file. Now that you've added scripts to the application with Script Assist mode, you can test the interactivity you've just added to it.

1. Select File > Save to save your FLA file.

2. Select Control > Test Movie.

3. Click any of the buttons (About, Products, Contact, and Home) to test that those frames are loading and that the corresponding title is displayed in the Title movie clip.

4. When you finish testing the application, close the SWF file by closing the test window.

You have now successfully added scripts to a button and both the main and `Title` movie clip timelines. You can use Script Assist mode in many ways as you work with ActionScript in your Flash documents.

Summary

Congratulations on using Script Assist mode to add scripts to objects and to the timeline. In just a few minutes, you learned how to accomplish the following tasks using Script Assist mode:

- Display Script Assist mode in the Actions panel and insert predefined ActionScript functions.

- Add a script to a button.

- Add frame scripts to the main timeline.

- Add a frame script to the last frame of a movie clip.

To learn more about ActionScript, take another lesson in the Basic ActionScript series.

ActionScript: Add Interactivity

19

Macromedia Flash Basic 8 and Macromedia Flash Professional 8 offer numerous ways to engage users with interactivity. When you incorporate interactivity, you're not limited to playing each frame in a timeline sequentially; however, sequential playing offers greater design and development options. This tutorial will show you some of the ways to implement interactivity in Flash.

You can print this tutorial by downloading a PDF version of it from the Macromedia Flash Documentation page at www.macromedia.com/go/fl_documentation.

In this tutorial, you will complete the following tasks:

> **NOTE**
> If you have Flash Professional 8, you can use screens to create a document. Screens provide additional navigation options. Slide screens, for example, already include built-in navigation that allows users to use keyboard arrow keys to move through screens. For more information about screens, select Help › Flash Tutorials › Basic Tasks: Create a Presentation with Screens (Flash Professional Only).

Set up your workspace

First, you'll open the start file for the lesson and set up your workspace to use an optimal layout for taking lessons.

1. To open your start file, in Flash select File > Open and navigate to the file:

   - In Windows, browse to *boot drive*\Program Files\ Macromedia\ Flash 8\Samples and Tutorials\Tutorial Assets\ActionScript\ Add Interactivity and double-click interactivity_start.fla.

   - On the Macintosh, browse to *Macintosh HD*/Applications/ Macromedia Flash 8/Samples and Tutorials/Tutorial Assets/ ActionScript/Add Interactivity and double-click interactivity_start.fla.

   The document opens in the Flash authoring environment.

2. Select File > Save As and save the document with a new name, in the same folder, to preserve the original start file.

   As you complete this lesson, remember to save your work frequently.

3. Select Window > Workspace Layout > Default to configure your workspace.

4. In the Stage View pop-up menu, in the upper-right side of the Timeline, select Show Frame to view both the Stage and the workspace.

5. Click in the workspace, away from objects on the Stage, so that no objects are selected.

Name button instances

You'll provide instance names for the buttons on the Stage so that you can refer to the instance names in ActionScript.

1. On the lower-right side of the Stage, select the button at the left.

   In the Property inspector (Window > Properties > Properties), type **goScene_btn** in the Instance Name text box to name the instance of the symbol.

2. Select the middle button and use the Property inspector to give the button an instance name of **attachMovie_btn**.

3. Select the far-right button and use the Property inspector to give the button an instance name of **playSound_btn**.

Add a scene

You can use scenes in Flash to organize your document into discrete sections that can contain content exclusive of other scenes. You'll create and add content to a new scene.

1. Select Insert > Scene.

   You can no longer see Scene 1, and Scene 2 now appears above the Stage. The Stage is empty.

2. From the Library panel (Window > Library), drag the Animation movie clip to the Stage.

   With the movie clip selected, use the Property inspector to give the instance an *x* coordinate of **200** and a *y* coordinate of **15**. Press Enter (Windows) or Return (Macintosh).

   The movie clip moves to the designated Stage coordinates.

3. Use the Property inspector to give the Animation movie clip an instance name of **animation_mc**.

4. Rename Layer 1 **Animation**.

   Create a new layer and name it **Buttons**. Drag an instance of the BTNback symbol to the Stage, and place it anywhere to the right of the movie clip.

5. Use the Property inspector to give the button an instance name of **back_btn**.

Move between scenes

You can move between scenes in the authoring environment by selecting a scene in the Scene panel.

1. To open the Scene panel, select Window > Other Panels > Scene.

2. Select Scene 1.

Control the document with a stop() action

When you test or publish a Flash document that contains more than one scene, by default the scenes play linearly, in the order in which they appear in the Scenes panel. You'll use a `stop()` action for Scene 1 so that the playhead in the Timeline stops at Frame 1 of Scene 1.

1. In the main Timeline for Scene 1, add a new layer and name it **Actions**.

2. Click Frame 1 of the Actions layer.

   In the Script pane of the Actions panel (Window > Actions), type the following comment followed by the script that stops the playhead on the frame:

```
// Stops the playhead at Frame 1.
stop();
```

Link a button to a scene

Now that the playhead stops at Frame 1, you'll add ActionScript that takes the user to Scene 2 upon releasing the goScene_btn instance.

- Press Enter (Windows) or Return (Macintosh) twice and type the following comment. Then write the function that takes users to Scene 2 upon release of the goScene_btn instance:

```
// This script takes the user to Scene 2 when goScene_btn
// is released.
goScene_btn.onRelease = function (){
  gotoAndStop("Scene 2", 1);
};
```

In the script that you just typed, you used the onRelease() method for the button object. The gotoAndStop() function is a timeline control function that lets you specify the scene and frame number. In this case, you specified Frame 1.

Add navigation to return to Scene 1

The function that you'll add to the button in Scene 2, to return the user to Scene 1, is similar to the function that you wrote to take the user to Scene 2.

1. In the Scene panel, select Scene 2.

   In the Timeline, create a new layer and name it **Actions**.

2. Select Frame 1 of the Actions layer.

   In the Actions panel, enter the following in the Script pane:

```
// function takes user to Scene 1 when back_btn instance
// is released
back_btn.onRelease = function (){
  gotoAndStop("Scene 1", 1);
  };
```

The only differences between this function and the function in Scene 1 are the name of the button and the name of the scene.

3. In the Scene panel, select Scene 1.

Play a movie clip

You can configure your document to play a movie clip at runtime. Using the `attachMovie()` method, you can attach an instance of a movie clip in the Library panel to the Stage even though you have not placed an instance on the Stage.

With the `attachMovie()` method, you must export the symbol for ActionScript and assign it a unique linkage identifier, which is different from the instance name.

1. In the Library panel, right-click the MCTrio symbol and select Linkage from the context menu.

2. In the Linkage Properties dialog box, select Export for ActionScript.

3. In the Identifier text box, verify that MCTrio appears as the linkage name.

4. Verify that Export in First Frame is selected, and then click OK.

    Movie clips that are exported for use with ActionScript load, by default, before the first frame of the SWF file that contains them. This can create a delay before the first frame plays. When you assign a linkage identifier to an element, you can specify that the movie clip loads on the first frame to avoid playback delays.

Use the attachMovie() method to play a movie clip

You'll now use the `attachMovie()` method to load the movie clip and provide the symbol with an instance name. Since the instance of the symbol does not exist on the Stage, you'll create the instance name programmatically.

1. In the Timeline, select Frame 1 of the Actions layer for Scene 1.

2. In the Script pane of the Actions panel, place the insertion point at the end of your last line of code.

    Press Enter (Windows) or Return (Macintosh), and then type the following to add a comment and create a new function:

    ```
    // function plays trio_mc when attachMovie_btn instance
    // is released
    attachMovie_btn.onRelease = function(){
    ```

Next, you'll specify what the function does: it plays the movie clip on the root Timeline, which is the main timeline. In your script, you'll refer to the movie clip by the linkage identifier name in the Linkage Properties dialog box (MCTrio).

Additionally, even though you didn't place an instance of the MCTrio symbol on the Stage, you'll use ActionScript to create an instance name for the symbol. The instance name that you'll specify is trio_mc.

3. With the insertion point at the end of the last line of script, press Enter or Return. Then type the following:

```
this._parent.attachMovie("MCTrio", "trio_mc", 1);
```

The number 1 in the script that you just typed refers to the depth on the layer in which to play the movie clip.

Every movie clip instance has its own *z* axis (depth) that determines the stacking order of a movie clip within its parent SWF file or movie clip. When you use the attachMovie() method to create a new movie clip at runtime, you always specify a depth for the new clip as a method parameter.

> **NOTE** For more information about the attachMovie() method, see attachMovie() in the *ActionScript 2.0 Language Reference*. Additionally, you can use the *ActionScript 2.0 Language Reference* for information about ActionScript that allows you to manage depth; getNextHighestDepth(), getDepth(), getInstanceAtDepth() are methods of the MovieClip class. The DepthManager class allows you to manage the relative depth assignments of a movie clip.

Specify movie clip Stage coordinates

In addition to the *z* axis for the movie clip, you must specify the *x* and *y* coordinates to place the movie clip within the Stage area at runtime.

■ Press Enter (Windows) or Return (Macintosh) after the last line in the Script pane and type the following:

```
trio_mc._x = 275;
trio_mc._y = 200;
};
```

Unload the movie clip

After the movie clip plays, you need a way to remove the movie clip from the Stage when the user goes to Scene 2. You can modify your script for the goScene_btn to "unload" the movie clip.

1. In the Timeline, select Frame 1 of the Actions layer.

   Then click at the end of the following line of script in the Script pane, within the function that takes the user to Scene 2, to place the insertion point:

   ```
   gotoAndStop("Scene 2", 1);
   ```

2. Press Enter (Windows) or Return (Macintosh) and type the following script, which unloads the movie clip when the function runs, so that the movie clip does not continue to play when the user goes to Scene 2:

   ```
   unloadMovie("trio_mc");
   ```

Your entire function for the goScene_btn should appear as follows:

```
// This script takes user to Scene 2 when goScene_btn
// instance is released.
goScene_btn.onRelease = function() {
  gotoAndStop("Scene 2", 1);
  unloadMovie("trio_mc");
};
```

Your entire script should appears as follows:

```
// Stops the playhead at Frame 1.
stop();

// This script takes user to Scene 2 when goScene_btn
// instance is released.
goScene_btn.onRelease = function (){
  gotoAndStop("Scene 2", 1);
  unloadMovie("trio_mc");
};

// This function plays trio_mc when attachMovie_btn
// instance is released.
attachMovie_btn.onRelease = function(){
this._parent.attachMovie("MCTrio", "trio_mc", 1);
trio_mc._x = 275;
trio_mc._y = 200;
```

Use a behavior to play an MP3 file

When you want to add interactivity to your document with ActionScript, you can often rely on behaviors to add the ActionScript for you. You'll use a sound behavior to play an MP3 file from the library.

1. In the Library panel, right-click (Windows) or Control-click (Macintosh) ping.mp3 and select Linkage from the context menu.

2. In the Linkage Properties dialog box, select Export for ActionScript and verify that Export in First Frame is selected.

3. Verify that ping.mp3 appears in the Identifier text box, and click OK.

4. On the Stage, select the playSound_btn instance.

5. In the Behaviors panel (Window > Behaviors), click Add (+) and select Sound > Load Sound from Library.

6. In the linkage ID text box, enter **ping.mp3**, and in the Name text box below, enter **ping**.

   Then click OK.

Test your document

Test your document to verify that the interactivity works as expected.

1. Select Control > Test Movie.

2. In the SWF file, click the left button to play Scene 2.

   When you finish viewing Scene 2, click Back.

3. Click the middle button in Scene 1 to see the movie clip play.

4. Click the right button to play the MP3 sound.

5. Click the left button again to verify that the movie clip unloads.

Summary

Congratulations on learning how to create an interactive document. In a few minutes, you learned how to accomplish the following tasks:

- Create a new scene.
- Write ActionScript to navigate between scenes.
- Write ActionScript to play an animated movie clip at runtime.
- Use a behavior to play an MP3 file.

To learn more about ActionScript, take another lesson in the Basic ActionScript series.

ActionScript: Write Scripts

20

The ActionScript language that is part of Macromedia Flash Basic 8 and Macromedia Flash Professional 8 offers designers and developers a variety of benefits. With ActionScript you can control document playback in response to events such as elapsed time and loading data; add interactivity to a document in response to user actions, such as a button click; use built-in objects, such as a button object, with built-in associated methods, properties, and events; create custom classes and objects; and create more compact and efficient applications than you could create using user interface tools, all with code that you can reuse.

ActionScript is an object-oriented scripting language that offers control over how your Flash content plays. In subsequent lessons, you'll see how ActionScript has evolved into ActionScript 2.0 to comprise a core set of language elements that make it easier to develop object-oriented programs.

You can print this tutorial by downloading a PDF version of it from the Macromedia Flash Documentation page at www.macromedia.com/go/fl_documentation.

In this tutorial, you will complete the following tasks:

Set up your workspace

First, you'll open the start file for the lesson and set up your workspace to use an optimal layout for taking lessons.

1. To open your start file, in Flash select File > Open and navigate to the file:

    ■ In Windows, browse to *boot drive*\Program Files\ Macromedia\Flash 8\Samples and Tutorials\Tutorial Assets\ ActionScript\Write Scripts and double-click scripts_start.fla.

    ■ On the Macintosh, browse to *Macintosh HD*/Applications/ Macromedia Flash 8/Samples and Tutorials/Tutorial Assets/ ActionScript/Write Scripts and double-click scripts_start.fla.

> **NOTE**
> The Write Scripts folder contains completed versions of the tutorial FLA files for your reference.

2. Select File > Save As and save the document with a new name, in the same folder, to preserve the original start file.

3. Select Window > Workspace Layout > Default to set up your workspace for taking lessons.

Create an instance of a symbol

You'll drag an instance of an animated movie clip from the library to the Global Positioning System artwork on the Stage. You'll then follow the recommended practice of always naming instances—both to prompt code hinting and because in your scripts you generally refer to instance names rather than symbol names. Code hints are the tooltips that prompt you with the correct ActionScript syntax.

1. In the Tools panel, click the Selection tool. Select the map layer in the Timeline, and click the padlock next to the map layer to unlock that layer.

2. To place the movie clip accurately, select View > Snapping. Select Snap Align and Snap to Objects if the commands are not already selected.

3. From the Library panel (Window > Library), drag map_skewed to the black background area of the Stage.

   Because guides don't appear when you first drag an object from the Library panel, you'll release the object, and then drag it again.

4. Drag the map_skewed movie clip on the Stage again so that the align guides appear. Use the guides to align the movie clip to the top and left edges of the GPS screen.

5. With the instance of map_skewed selected on the Stage, type **screen_mc** in the Instance Name text box of the Property inspector (Window > Properties).

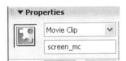

   Flash is designed to present code hints when you name your instances with the appropriate suffix:

   ■ When naming a movie clip instance, always give the instance a suffix of _mc, as in screen_mc.

   ■ When naming a button, use the _btn suffix.

   ■ When naming a text field, use the _txt suffix.

Name button instances

Using the appropriate suffix to prompt code hinting, you'll provide instance names for two button instances that are already on the Stage.

1. In the Timeline, unlock the Buttons layer.

2. On the Stage, select the instance of play_button (the large green button).

3. In the Instance Name text box of the Property inspector, type **onButton_btn** to name the instance.

4. On the Stage, select the instance of button_stop (the small red button).

5. In the Instance Name text box of the Property inspector, type **offButton_btn** to name the instance.

Initialize the document

Applications have an initial state that specifies how the content first appears to users. You initialize properties and variables in the first frame of a document. You'll specify that the map movie clip should not be visible when the SWF file first plays.

1. Select Frame 1 of the Actions layer. If the Actions panel isn't open, select Window > Actions.

   Actions - Frame appears at the top of the panel, which indicates that you selected a frame in which to apply ActionScript. It's a good practice to verify that you're attaching ActionScript to the intended frame or object.

   The Actions panel includes a Script pane, the blank text entry area, in which you can enter text directly; an Actions toolbox, which lets you select ActionScript to add to your script; and a Script navigator, which functions like the Movie Explorer.

 2. Along the top of the Actions panel, click Insert Target path.

3. In the Insert Target Path dialog box, verify that Relative, meaning relative path, is selected. From the hierarchical tree in the dialog box, select screen_mc. Click OK.

   A target path tells ActionScript the location of an object within the overall structure of a document. For more information about paths, see "Using absolute and relative target paths" in Flash Help.

4. Click in the Script pane, at the end of the screen_mc text, and type a period (.).

5. When you type the period, code hints appear for the movie clip, because you used the _mc suffix when naming the instance. Double-click `_visible` from the list of code hints, and type the following:

`= false;`

This line of code makes the screen_mc movie clip invisible on the Stage.

> **NOTE**
>
> If code hints don't appear, you don't have code hints selected as a preference in the Actions panel. You can type `_visible` directly in the Script pane. You can also change your preferences by clicking the pop-up menu in the upper-right corner of the Actions panel. From the pop-up menu, select Preferences, and then select Code Hints on the ActionScript tab.

Throughout authoring, remember to save your document frequently.

Apply ActionScript syntax

All languages, whether computer languages or written and spoken "human" languages, follow specific rules that foster comprehension. These rules are known as the language syntax.

Flash uses dot syntax, which means that the period (.) links parts of a script. Other ActionScript syntax elements include the following:

- A semicolon (;) in an ActionScript statement, like a period in an ordinary sentence, indicates the end of a statement.

- Parentheses () group arguments that apply to an ActionScript statement.

- Curly braces {} group related ActionScript statements. You can use nested braces to create a hierarchy of statements.

Later in this lesson, you'll use Flash features that allow you to test your syntax.

Locate ActionScript reference documentation

During authoring, if you'd like additional information about the ActionScript that you enter, you can select the action in the Actions toolbox or Script pane and click Reference. The Help panel displays information about the selected action.

1. In the Script pane of the Actions panel, double-click `visible` to select the term.

> **NOTE** After completing the next step, you'll change topics in the Help panel and you will no longer be on this lesson topic. In the Help panel, click the History Back icon to return to this topic.

2. Along the top of the Actions panel, click the Help icon.

   The `visible` entry in the Help panel appears.

Add comments to ActionScript

In ActionScript, text after double slashes (//) is commented text, which Macromedia Flash Player ignores. Commented text often documents script functionality so that other developers can understand your script, but you can also use comments to deactivate sections of your script when debugging. As a best practice, always add comments that explain your scripts.

- In the Script pane of the Actions panel, place the insertion point at the beginning of the line of code and type `// Initialize document to hide screen movie clip`. Press Enter (Windows) or Return (Macintosh).

  Text in the Script pane appears as follows:

  ```
  // Initialize document to hide screen movie clip.
  this.screen_mc._visible = false;
  ```

> **NOTE** If your commented text is many lines, you can use /* instead of double slashes for the beginning of the comment, and */ to mark the end of the comment.

Write a function for a button

A command in ActionScript is called a function. A function is a script that you can write once and use repeatedly in a document to perform a certain task. You're going to write a function that makes the screen_mc movie clip appear (visible = true) when the user releases the mouse button.

1. In the Script pane of the Actions panel, click after the last line of code, press Enter (Windows) or Return (Macintosh) twice, and type //
   ```
   function to show animation
   ```

2. Press Enter or Return and click Insert Target Path, along the top of the Actions panel. Select onButton_btn from the hierarchical tree, and click OK.

3. In the Script pane, type a period (.) and double-click onRelease from the list of code hints that appears.

4. In the Script pane, press the Spacebar and type the following:
   ```
   = function(){
   ```
   The line of code that you just completed should appear as follows:
   ```
   this.onButton_btn.onRelease = function(){
   ```

   You already know how to select objects in the Insert Target Path dialog box; you'll now enter the instance names directly into the Script pane.

5. Press Enter or Return, and type the following:
   ```
   screen_mc._visible = true;
   ```

6. Press Enter or Return and type } ; to specify the end of the statement.

   The function should appear as follows:
   ```
   // function to show animation
   this.onButton_btn.onRelease = function(){
     screen_mc._visible = true;
   };
   ```

Copy and modify a button function

You just created one function that sets the visible property of a movie clip to true when the user releases the mouse button after a button click. You can probably guess how to create another function that hides the screen_mc movie clip: by setting the movie clip _visible property to false when the user clicks an Off button. You'll create that function now.

1. In the Script pane, select the entire function that you just typed, including the comment, curly brackets, and semicolon. Copy the text as you normally would, using Control+C (Windows) or Command+C (Macintosh).

2. In the Script pane, place the insertion point after the last line of code. Then press Enter (Windows) or Return (Macintosh) twice, and paste the text as you normally would, using Control+V (Windows) or Command+V (Macintosh).

3. In the copied function, change the text in onButton_btn to read offButton_btn.

   Remember, earlier you assigned an instance name of offButton_btn to an instance.

4. In the copied function, change the visible property of the screen_mc movie clip from true to false.

5. In the copied function, change the commented text after the slashes to read function to hide animation.

   Your entire script should appear as follows:

```
// Initialize document to hide screen movie clip.
this.screen_mc._visible = false;

// function to show animation
this.onButton_btn.onRelease = function(){
  screen_mc._visible = true;
};

// function to hide animation
this.offButton_btn.onRelease = function(){
  screen_mc._visible = false;
};
```

Check syntax and test your application

As you learned earlier in this lesson, ActionScript depends on correct syntax to execute properly. Flash offers a variety of ways for you to test your syntax.

1. To check the syntax, do one of the following:

   - Click the pop-up menu in the upper-right corner of the Actions panel title bar and select Check Syntax.

   - Click Check Syntax along the top of the Actions panel.

   If the syntax is correct, a message appears stating that the script contains no errors.

   If the syntax is incorrect, a message appears stating the script contains errors; the Output panel opens and displays information about the error.

2. Click OK to close the syntax message.

3. After you've verified that your ActionScript does not contain syntax errors, save the document and select Control > Test Movie.

   When the SWF file appears, the animation should not appear in the Global Positioning System screen, because its initial `visible` property is set to `false`. When you click and release the top green button, you call the function that sets the movie clip's `visible` property to `true`. Does the animation play then? Finally, click the red Off button to see if the `visible` property for the animation is again `false`.

   You can test your SWF content throughout authoring to confirm that it plays as expected.

Summary

Congratulations on learning a few basics about writing scripts with ActionScript. In a short amount of time, you learned how to accomplish the following tasks:

- Name instances following recommended practices.
- Initialize a document.
- Apply ActionScript syntax.
- Locate ActionScript reference documentation.
- Add comments to ActionScript.
- Write a function.
- Copy and modify a function.
- Check syntax and test your application.

To learn more about ActionScript, select Help > Flash Tutorials > Basic Tasks: Create an Application.

CHAPTER 21

ActionScript: Create a Form with Conditional Logic and Send Data

You can create a form with conditional logic that allows the SWF file to respond to user interaction and send the form data from the SWF file to an external source. This tutorial shows you how to create a simple form.

Before taking this lesson, you should be familiar with writing functions and variables; to learn about these, select Help > Flash Tutorials > Basic Tasks: Create an Application.

You can print this tutorial by downloading a PDF version of it from the Macromedia Flash Documentation page at www.macromedia.com/go/fl_documentation.

In this tutorial, you will complete the following tasks:

Set up your workspace

First, you'll open the start file for the lesson and set up your workspace to use an optimal layout for taking lessons.

1. To open your start file, in Flash select File > Open and navigate to the file:

   - In Windows, browse to *boot drive*\Program Files\ Macromedia\ Flash 8\Samples and Tutorials\Tutorial Assets\ActionScript\ Create a Form and double-click simpleForm_start.fla.

   - On the Macintosh, browse to *Macintosh HD*/Applications/ Macromedia Flash 8/Samples and Tutorials/Tutorial Assets/ ActionScript/Create a Form and double-click simpleForm_start.fla.

> **NOTE** The Create a Form folder contains completed versions of the tutorial FLA files for your reference.

2. Select File > Save As and save the document with a new name, in the same folder, to preserve the original start file.

3. Select Window > Workspace Layout > Default to set up your workspace for taking lessons.

4. If necessary, drag the lower edge of the timeline (Window > Timeline) down to enlarge the timeline view.

Add an input text field to collect form data

You'll start by inserting a text field in your document in which viewers can enter data. You will also name the text field so you can later reference the text field as you use ActionScript in your Flash application.

1. Click in the workspace, away from objects on the Stage, so that no objects are selected.

2. In the Tools panel, select the Text tool.

3. In the Property inspector, do the following to set text attributes:

  ■ Select Input Text from the Text Type pop-up menu.

  ■ Select _sans from the Font pop-up menu.

  ■ Enter **10** in the Font Size text box.

  ■ Click the text color box and select a shade of dark blue.

  ■ Verify that Align Left is selected.

  ■ Verify that Single Line is selected in the Line Type pop-up menu.

4. In the Timeline, select Frame 1 of the Input Text layer.

5. On the Stage, drag the Text tool to create an input text field to the right of the http:// text.

6. If necessary, use the Selection tool to drag the text field or use the arrows keys to adjust the position.

7. With the input text field still selected, in the Property inspector, type **url_txt** in the Instance Name text box.

  You'll refer to the instance name later when you add ActionScript.

Add a Submit button to the form

The Library panel contains a Submit button symbol that you will add to the form.

1. From the Library panel (Window > Library), drag the Submit button to the Stage and place it over the SubmitURL guide.

http://
⊕
Submit URL

2. Drag the button or use the arrows keys to adjust the position, if necessary.

3. In the Property inspector, type **submit_btn** in the Instance Name text box.

Add an error message

You'll add a message to display if the user clicks the Submit button before entering data.

1. In the Timeline, with the Branding layer selected, click Insert Layer and name the layer **Dialog Boxes**.

2. Select Frame 5 of the Dialog Boxes layer.

   Right-click (Windows) or Control-click (Macintosh) the selected layer and select Insert Blank Keyframe from the context menu.

3. From the Library panel, drag the `Dialog Box-error` movie clip to the center of the Stage.

4. In the Timeline, select Frame 5 of the Buttons layer.

5. Drag the Try Again Button symbol from the Library panel to the Stage, placing the button below the error message text.

6. With the button still selected, in the Property inspector, enter **tryAgain_btn** in the Instance Name text box.

Add a confirmation message

Next, you'll add a message to display when the user submits an entry in the text field.

1. In the Dialog Boxes layer, select Frame 10.

    Right-click (Windows) or Control-click (Macintosh) the selected frame and select Insert Blank Keyframe from the context menu.

2. From the Library panel, drag the `Dialog Box-confirm` movie clip to the center of the Stage.

3. Close the Library panel.

Add a stop() action

When a Flash application loads in Flash Player, it automatically plays in a continuous loop. You use ActionScript to control playhead movement in a timeline. You will add a `stop()` action in the first frame of your application so the user can make an entry in the input text field.

1. In the Timeline, with the Input Text layer selected, add a new layer and name it **Actions**.

2. Select Frame 1 of the Actions layer.

3. In the Actions panel (Window > Actions), verify that Frame 1 is selected.

4. Click in the Script pane of the Actions panel, and type the following comment:

`// Stops the playhead at Frame 1.`

Press Enter (Windows) or Return (Macintosh).

5. Type `stop();` to add the stop action.

Add frame labels for navigation

When the viewer presses the Submit button, you want Flash to jump to either the error message or the confirmation message, depending on what is entered in the text field. Labeling a frame helps you reference it in ActionScript easily. This is helpful for sending the playhead to a specific frame.

Next, you'll add frame labels to help you navigate your Flash application.

1. Add a keyframe (Insert > Timeline > Keyframe) to Frame 5 of the Actions layer.

2. In the Property inspector, type **error** in the Frame Label text box.

Press Enter (Windows) or Return (Macintosh). The label text and a flag appear in Frame 5 of the Timeline.

3. Add a keyframe to Frame 10 of the Actions layer.

In the Property inspector, type **confirm** in the Frame Label text box. Press Enter or Return.

Add conditional logic for the Submit button

With ActionScript, you can have Flash compare information and take action based on criteria you specify. In this example, you'll add ActionScript for Flash to take one action if the user enters no data in the text field, and a different action if the user does enter data.

1. Select Frame 1 of the Actions layer.

   In the Script pane, place the insertion point after the `stop()`; code. Press Enter (Windows) or Return (Macintosh).

2. Type the following comment:

   ```
   // Adds conditional logic for the Submit button that
   // validates user input.
   ```

   Press Enter or Return.

 3. In the Actions panel, click Insert a Target Path, located at the top of the panel.

4. In the Insert Target Path dialog box, verify that Relative is selected.

   Click submit_btn on the hierarchical tree, and click OK.

5. In the Script pane, type a period (.) after `submit_btn`, and then type `onRelease`.

6. With the insertion point after `onRelease`, type `= function (){}` in the Script pane.

7. Place the insertion point between the curly braces and press Enter or Return, and then type `if (url_txt.text == null || url_txt.text == ""){` in the Script pane.

   The parallel lines are equivalent to logical *or* in ActionScript.

8. With the insertion point still inside the curly braces, press Enter or Return.

9. Type `gotoAndStop("error");` in the Script pane.

   Press Enter or Return.

10. Place the insertion point after the curly brace and type `else{` in the Script pane.

    Press Enter or Return.

11. Type `gotoAndStop("confirm")` in the Script pane.

Press Enter or Return, and type }, and then press Enter or Return again and type };. Your script should appear as follows:

```
// Stops the playhead at Frame 1.
stop();
// Adds conditional logic for the Submit button that
// validates user input.
this.submit_btn.onRelease = function(){
  if (url_txt.text == null || url_txt.text ==""){
    gotoAndStop("error");
} else {
    gotoAndStop("confirm")
  }
};
```

Pass data out of a SWF file

You can send data from a Flash application in various ways—for example, in this lesson you send data to a web server to load a web page in the browser. After the `else` statement, you'll add the ActionScript to have Flash go to the URL the viewer enters in the input text field.

1. In the Script pane, place the insertion point in front of the line that reads `gotoAndStop("confirm")`.

2. In the Actions toolbox, select Global Functions > Browser/Network and double-click `getURL`.

3. With the insertion point between the `getURL()` parentheses, type `"http://"+url_txt.text` to specify the data that should pass from the SWF file.

(Do not leave spaces in the code.) Your script should look like the following:

```
stop();
this.submit_btn.onRelease = function(){
  if (url_txt.text == null || url_txt.text ==""){
    gotoAndStop("Error");
} else {
    getUrl ("http://"+url_txt.text);
    gotoAndStop("Confirm")
  }
};
```

Write a function for the Try Again button

A function is a script that you can use repeatedly to perform a specific task. You can pass parameters to a function, and it can return a value. In this example, when the user clicks the Try Again button, a function runs that returns the playhead to Frame 1.

You'll write that function now. In this script, you'll type the frame number, because you did not label Frame 1.

1. In the Timeline, select Frame 5 of the Actions layer.

2. In the Script pane, type the following comment:

    ```
    // button function returns user to Frame 1.
    ```

    Press Enter (Windows) or Return (Macintosh).

3. Type `tryAgain_btn.onRelease = function(){`, and then press Enter or Return.

4. Type `gotoAndStop(1);`, and then press Enter or Return and type } to complete the script.

Test your SWF file

You'll test your document by entering a URL and checking whether it works as expected.

1. Select Control > Test Movie.

2. When the SWF file appears, click Submit before typing anything in the input text field.

    The error message appears.

3. Click Try Again, and then type the URL of a valid website in the input text field.

    Click Submit.

    Your default browser opens the web page.

Summary

Congratulations on learning how to write a script with conditional logic and send data. In a few minutes, you learned how to complete the following tasks:

- Add an input text field to a document.
- Create a button symbol.
- Add a `stop()` action.
- Write a script that validates the form with conditional logic.
- Pass data out of a SWF file.
- Write a function.

To learn more about Flash, take another lesson.

ActionScript: Work with Objects and Classes

22

Classes are the blueprint for objects in Macromedia Flash Basic 8 and Macromedia Flash Professional 8. All objects in Flash have an underlying class; for example, all movie clips have a method called `getURL()`, and `getURL()` is defined in the class definition for a movie clip. Flash contains many predefined classes, such as the MovieClip class, the Array class, the Color class, and the CheckBox class. This tutorial will show you how to create and modify classes.

You can print this tutorial by downloading a PDF version of it from the Macromedia Flash Documentation page at www.macromedia.com/go/fl_documentation.

In this tutorial, you will complete the following tasks:

> **NOTE**
>
> This tutorial is designed for Flash developers who are familiar with basic Flash and ActionScript concepts.

Set up your workspace

First, you'll view the finished files and set up your workspace to use an optimal layout for taking lessons.

1. View the finished files.

   This lesson does not include start files. You can find finished files of handson1.fla, handson2.fla, handson3.fla, Product.as, and Drag.as, which are examples of the files that you'll create in this lesson:

   - In Windows, browse to *boot drive*\Program Files\ Macromedia\ Flash 8\Samples and Tutorials\ Tutorial Assets\ActionScript\ Work with Objects and Classes.

   - On the Macintosh, browse to *Macintosh HD*/Applications/ Macromedia Flash 8/Samples and Tutorials/Tutorial Assets/ ActionScript/Work with Objects and Classes.

2. Select Window > Workspace Layout > Default to configure your workspace.

Learn about classes and object types

A *class,* also referred to as an *object type,* is like a blueprint. An object doesn't exist until you create it, or instantiate it, from a class definition. An object is an instance of a class.

Properties are the characteristics of an object. For example, when you align movie clips, you change the _x and _y properties of the MovieClip object. A property is a variable that is attached to a class. A property can either be public, which means it is accessible outside the class, or private, which means it can be accessed only within the class.

In object-oriented terms, a method is a behavior or procedure that can act on the object. A hypothetical throw( ) method on a ball would know the size and weight of the ball. A method is aware of the object and all the properties that it contains and can work on that object.

Create an object from a class

You'll create an existing class using visual tools (the TextField class) and code (using the Date class).

1. Open a new Flash document and change the name of Layer 1 to **Text**.

2. In the Text layer, create a dynamic text field and assign it the instance name of **currentDate_txt**.

3. Create an Actions layer.

   With Frame 1 of the Actions layer selected, open the Actions panel.

4. Create, or instantiate, an object from the Date class, named **myDate**:

   ```
   var myDate:Date=new Date();
   ```

5. Create a variable called **currentMonth** equal to the `getMonth()` method:

   ```
   var currentMonth:Number = myDate.getMonth();
   ```

6. Trace the value of `currentMonth`:

   ```
   trace (currentMonth);
   ```

7. Save and test the document.

   You should see a number in the Output panel that represents the month.

   The `getMonth()` method displays the current month. The `getMonth()` method is zero-indexed, meaning the numbering begins at zero rather than one, so the number displayed is one less than what you would expect.

8. Close the Output panel and the SWF file window.

Modify your script

You'll modify your script to compensate for the zero indexing.

1. Add **+1** to the value when you create `currentMonth`, and test your document to be sure the expected month number appears.

   That line of script should read as follows:

   ```
   var currentMonth:Number = myDate.getMonth()+1;
   ```

2. Comment the trace statement:

   ```
   // trace (currentMonth);
   ```

3. Below the trace statement, set the `autoSize` property of your text box to `true`:

   ```
   currentDate_txt.autoSize = true;
   ```

4. Use the text property of your text box to display today's date in the form Today is mm/dd/yyyy.

   Use the `currentMonth` variable you already created, plus the `getDate()` and `getFullYear()` methods of the Date object:

   ```
   currentDate_txt.text="Today is "+currentMonth+"/"+
      myDate.getDate() + "/"+myDate.getFullYear();
   ```

5. Verify that your script appears as follows:

   ```
   var myDate:Date=new Date();
   var currentMonth:Number = myDate.getMonth()+1;
   // trace (currentMonth);
   currentDate_txt.autoSize = true;
   currentDate_txt.text="Today is "+currentMonth+"/"+
      myDate.getDate() + "/"+myDate.getFullYear();
   ```

6. Save and test the document.

   The current date should appear in the SWF file window.

NOTE | A finished sample file of the document you just created, named handson1.fla, is located in your finished files folder. For the path, see "Set up your workspace" on page 256.

Create a custom class

Although ActionScript includes many classes of objects, such as the MovieClip class and the Color class, there will be times when you need to construct your own classes so you can create objects based on a particular set of properties or methods.

To create a class that defines each of the new objects, you create a constructor for a custom object class and then create new object instances based on that new class, as in the following example:

> **NOTE** The following ActionScript is an example only. Do not enter the script in your lesson FLA file.

```
function Product (id:Number, prodName:String, price:Number)
{
  this.id = id;
  this.prodName = prodName;
  this.price = price;
}
```

To properly define a class in ActionScript 2.0, you must surround all classes by the `class` keyword, and you must declare all variables in the constructor outside of the constructor.

> **NOTE** The following ActionScript is an example only. Do not enter the script in your lesson FLA file.

```
class Product
{
  // variable declarations
  var id:Number
  var prodName:String
  var price:Number
  // constructor
  function Product (id:Number, prodName:String,
  price:Number){
    this.id  = id;
    this.prodName = prodName;
    this.price = price;
  }
}
```

To create objects from this class, you could now use the following code:

```
var cliplessPedal:Product=new Product(1, "Clipless Pedal",
    11);
var monkeyBar:Product=new Product(2, "Monkey Bar", 10);
```

However, in ActionScript 2.0, variables that are part of a class structure should not be accessed directly. Write methods within the class that will access these variables directly. Different methods should get and set properties (known as "getter" and "setter" methods). You must indicate the data type for both a method's return value and any parameters that are passed to the method when it is called.

Specify the data type for method return values

You must indicate data types for values returned by methods after the method name and list of parameters, as in the following example:

```
public function getProductName() :String
{
   return name;
}
```

If no value is returned (for example, a property is being set), the data type is Void:

```
public function setProductName(productName:String) :Void
{
   this.productName=productName;
}
```

Build a custom class

You'll now build a new Product class with getter and setter methods and create an object from the Product class.

1. Create an ActionScript file by selecting File > New > ActionScript File (Not Flash Document). Save the document with the name **Product.as**.

2. Create a constructor for a Product class by creating a function called Product that takes the arguments `id`, `prodName`, and `description`:

```
function Product (id:Number, prodName:String,
  description:String)
  {}
```

3. In the constructor function, set the properties of the Product class equal to the setter methods that you will create:

```
setID(id);
setProdName(prodName);
setDescription(description);
```

4. Surround the `class` keyword with the constructor function.

Declare each variable used in the class:

```
class Product
{
   var id:Number;
   var prodName:String;
   var description:String

   function Product (id:Number, prodName:String,
   description:String)
{
     setID(id);
     setProdName(prodName);
     setDescription(description);
}
}
```

5. Define getter and setter methods for each property of the class, as in the following example.

Specify `Void` as the return type for the setter methods, and indicate the data type returned for the getter methods.

```
class Product
{
     var id:Number;
     var prodName:String;
     var description:String
```

```
        function Product (id:Number, prodName:String,
    description:String) {
        setID(id);
        setProdName(prodName);
        setDescription(description);
    }

    public function setID (id:Number) :Void
    {

        this.id = id;
    }

    public function setProdName (prodName:String) :Void
    {

        this.prodName = prodName;
    }

    public function setDescription (description:String)
    :Void
    {

        this.description = description;
    }

    public function getID () :Number {
        return id;
    }

    public function getProdName () :String {
        return prodName
    }

    public function getDescription () :String {
        return description;
    }
}
```

6. Save your file.

> **NOTE** A finished sample file of the file you just created, named Product.as, is located in your finished files folder. For the path, see "Set up your workspace" on page 256.

Create two objects from the Product class

You'll create a new FLA file, and then create two objects from the Product class.

1. Open a new Flash document and save it in the same location where you saved Product.as.

2. In the new document, select Frame 1 in the Timeline.

3. In the Actions panel, create two objects from the Product class using the data shown in the following table (the ActionScript that you'll create appears after the table).

Instance name	Data	
pedals	id	0
	prodName	Clipless Pedals
	description	Excellent cleat engagement
handleBars	id	1
	prodName	ATB
	description	Available in comfort and aero design

4. Verify that you created the objects as follows:

```
var handleBars:Product = new Product (1, "ATB",
   "Available in comfort and aero design");
var pedals:Product=new Product(0,"Clipless
   Pedals","Excellent cleat engagement");
```

5. Trace the description property of pedals:

```
trace (pedals.getDescription ());
```

6. Save and test the document.

You should see the description of pedals in the Output panel.

> **NOTE** A finished sample file of the document you just created, named handson2.fla, is located in your finished files folder. For the path, see "Set up your workspace" on page 256.

Learn about extending existing classes

The extends keyword in ActionScript 2.0 allows you to use all the methods and properties of an existing class in a new class. For example, if you wanted to define a class called Drag that inherited everything from the MovieClip class, you could use the following:

```
class Drag extends MovieClip
{}
```

The Drag class now inherits all properties and methods from the existing MovieClip class, and you can use MovieClip properties and methods anywhere within the class definition, as in the following example:

> **NOTE** The following ActionScript is an example only. Do not enter the script in your lesson FLA file.

```
class Drag extends MovieClip
{
    // constructor
    function Drag ()
    {
      onPress=doDrag;
      onRelease=doDrop;
    }
    private function doDrag():Void
    {
      this.startDrag();
    }
    private function doDrop():Void
    {
      this.stopDrag();
    }
}
```

> **NOTE** The Convert to Symbol dialog box now offers a class field in which you can associate visual objects (such as movie clip) with any class that you define in ActionScript 2.0.

Extend the MovieClip class to create a new class

You'll create a new class by extending the built-in MovieClip class.

1. Create a new Flash document and name it **Shape.fla**.

2. Using the drawing tools, draw a shape on the Stage.

   With the entire shape selected, right-click (Windows) or Control-click (Macintosh) the shape and select Convert to Symbol from the context menu.

3. In the Convert to Symbol dialog box, select Movie Clip as the behavior, and click Advanced.

   Select Export for ActionScript.

4. In the Name text box, enter **myShape**.

5. In the AS 2.0 Class text box, enter **Drag**.

Click OK. This associates the movie clip with the Drag class that you'll create.

6. Using the Property inspector, assign the movie clip an instance name, then save the FLA file.

> **NOTE** A finished sample file of the document you just created, named handson3.fla, is located in your finished files folder. For the path, see "Set up your workspace" on page 256.

7. Create an ActionScript file by selecting File > New > ActionScript File (Not Flash Document). Save the document with the name **Drag.as**, in the same location where you saved Shape.fla.

8. In the ActionScript file that you just created, create a new class and constructor called `Drag`:

```
class Drag extends MovieClip
   {
      function Drag ()
      {
        onPress=doDrag;
   onRelease=doDrop;
      }
   }
```

9. Define private methods in the class that use the existing movie clip methods, `startDrag()` and `stopDrag()`:

```
class Drag extends MovieClip
   {
function Drag()
 {
   onPress=doDrag;
   onRelease=doDrop;
 }
private function doDrag():Void
 {
this.startDrag();
 }
private function doDrop():Void
 {
   this.stopDrag()
 }
 }
```

10. Save the ActionScript file.

11. Test the Shape.fla file.

You should be able to drag the movie clip.

> **NOTE**
>
> An example of the ActionScript file you just created, named Drag.as, is located in your finished files folder. For the path, see "Set up your workspace" on page 256.

Summary

Congratulations on learning how to work with objects and classes in ActionScript 2.0. In a few minutes, you learned how to accomplish the following tasks:

- Create and use objects from existing classes.
- Create a custom class.
- Create a property within a custom class.
- Create a method within a custom class.
- Extend an existing class and take advantage of inheritance.

CHAPTER 23

Data Integration: Overview (Flash Professional Only)

23

The following tutorials illustrate several ways to use data binding and the data components in Macromedia Flash Professional 8. Many of the tutorials use public web services and therefore require that you have an Internet connection. In addition, the tutorials won't work in a browser because of sandbox restrictions, but they will work in the Flash authoring environment or Flash Player.

- Data Integration: Using the Macromedia Tips Web Service (Flash Professional Only)

- Data Integration: Using XML for a Timesheet (Flash Professional Only)

- Data Integration: Using XUpdate to Update the Timesheet (Flash Professional Only)

> **NOTE**
>
> To complete the timesheet tutorials, you must download the file data.xml.

These tutorials are working models that illustrate how to use the data components (XMLConnector, WebServices Connector, RDMBSResolver and XUpdateResolver) with data binding in Flash Professional 8. They are not intended to be production-ready applications.

> **NOTE**
>
> The use of public web services in these tutorials does not imply that you should use them for real-world applications. In fact, Macromedia does not recommend using public web services directly from within any client-side application. For more information, see "Applications and Web Services" in the "Data Integration" chapter in *Using Flash* (in Flash, select Help › Using Flash).

If you have trouble downloading or decompressing the files, see TechNote 13686 at www.macromedia.com/support/general/ts/documents/downfiles.htm.

CHAPTER 24

Data Integration: Using the Macromedia Tips Web Service (Flash Professional Only)

24

In this tutorial, you use the Web Services panel to connect to a web service, which you use to return a random tip about Macromedia software. You then use components to set up a simple user interface.

You can print this tutorial by downloading a PDF version of it from the Macromedia Flash Documentation page at www.macromedia.com/go/fl_documentation.

In this tutorial, you will complete the following tasks:

This tutorial uses a public web service and therefore requires that you have an Internet connection.

If you have trouble downloading or decompressing the files, see TechNote 13686 at www.macromedia.com/support/general/ts/documents/downfiles.htm.

> **NOTE**
>
> The use of a public web service in this tutorial does not imply that you should use one for real-world applications. In fact, Macromedia does not recommend using public web services directly from within any client-side application. For more information, see "About data connectivity and security in Flash Player" in the "Data Integration" chapter in *Using Flash* (in Flash, select Help > Using Flash). In a production environment, you should use web services that are placed on your own web server.

The finished FLA file for this tutorial is installed with Flash. The following list provides the typical paths to this directory.

- In Windows, browse to *boot drive*\Program Files\Macromedia\ Flash 8\Samples and Tutorials\Tutorial Assets\Data Integration\Tips.

- On the Macintosh: browse to *Macintosh HD*/Applications/ Macromedia Flash 8/Samples and Tutorials/Tutorial Assets/ Data Integration/Tips.

Connect to a public web service

Define a web service in Flash that will connect to a public web service.

1. Create a new Flash document using Flash Professional 8. Make sure your computer is connected to the Internet.

2. Open the Web Services panel (Window > Other Panels > Web Services), and click Define Web Services.

3. In the Define Web Services dialog box that appears, click Add Web Service (+), and then click the highlighted line to edit it.

4. Enter the URL **http://www.flash-mx.com/mm/tips/tips.cfc?WSDL** and click OK.

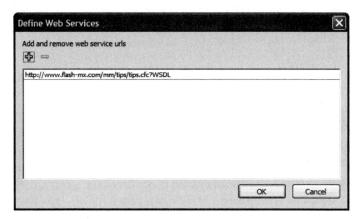

5. In the Web Services panel, inspect the methods, parameters, and results of the Macromedia Tips web service.

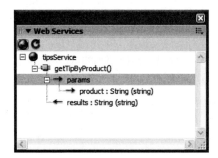

The web service has one method, called `getTipByProduct()`. This method accepts a single parameter called `product`. The parameter is a string that tells the web service what Macromedia product you want to see a tip for. In the next step, you bind this parameter with a ComboBox instance in your application.

6. Right-click the `getTipByProduct()` method, and select Add Method Call from the context menu.

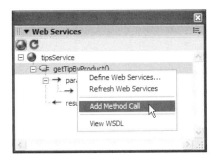

An instance of the WebServiceConnector component is added to the Stage.

7. In the Property inspector, enter the instance name **tips_wsc**.

The component is now configured and on the Stage. You can place the component anywhere on or off the Stage—it is invisible when you run the application.

Create a user interface and bind the components with the web service

Next, you use components to create a simple user interface that you can use to select a product, click a button, and see a random tip about the product. You create this application by binding the user interface components on the Stage to the parameters and returned results of the Macromedia Tips web service.

1. In the Components panel, select UI Components > ComboBox. Drag a ComboBox component to the Stage. In the Property inspector, enter the instance name **products_cb**.

2. In the Components panel, select UI Components > Button. Drag a Button component to the Stage. In the Property inspector, enter the instance name **submit_button** and for the label property type **Get Tip**, as follows:

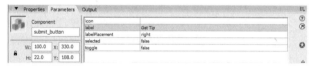

3. In the Components panel, select UI Components > TextArea. Drag the component onto the Stage. In the Property inspector, enter the instance name **tip_ta**.

4. In the Components panel, select UI Components > Label and drag a Label component onto the Stage. Place it above the ComboBox component.

5. In the Property inspector, in the Instance name field type **products_lbl** and for the text property type **Select a Product**, as follows:

The Property inspector showing the instance name products_lbl and the text "Select a Product"

6. Drag another Label component above the `tip_ta` TextArea component. In the Property inspector, give it the Instance name **tip_lbl** and in the text field type **Tips**.

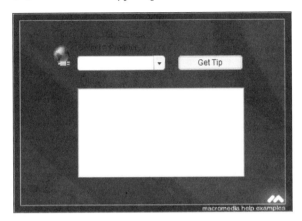

Now add a binding for the WebService connector component from the Macromedia Tip web service to ComboBox component that allows the user to choose a product and return a tip about the product.

7. Select the WebServiceConnector component on the Stage. Open the Component inspector and click the Bindings tab. Click Add Binding (+). In the Add Binding dialog box, select `product:String` (under `params:Object`) and click OK.

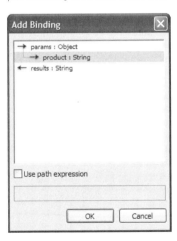

8. In the Component inspector, double-click the empty value in the Bound To field. In the Bound To dialog box, select `ComboBox`, `<products_cb>` for the component path and `value:String` for the schema location. Click OK.

Bound To field in the Component inspector

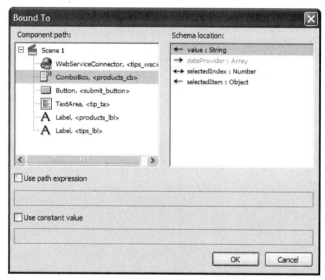

Selecting the component path and schema location in the Bound To dialog box

Next, you will bind the `results` parameter in the web service connector to the TextArea component on the Stage.

9. In the Component inspector, click Add Binding (+) again. In the Add Binding dialog box, select `results:String`, and then click OK. In the Component inspector, double-click the empty value in the Bound To field, and in the Bound To dialog box, select `TextArea, <tip_ta>` as the component path and `text:String` as the schema location. Click OK.

Finally, you will use a Button component and the `trigger()` method to trigger the service. You use the trigger method to attempt to retrieve a tip whenever you click the button.

10. Open the Actions panel and add the following ActionScript on Frame 1 of the Timeline:

```
submit_button.onRelease = function(){
    tips_wsc.trigger();
};
```

11. Next, add the following ActionScript after the code from step 10. The code uses the `dataProvider` property to set the items in the ComboBox instance to the contents of the array.

```
products_cb.dataProvider = ["Flash", "Dreamweaver"];
```

> **NOTE** If necessary, you can use the `setStyle()` method to change the color of the Label instance text to white using
> `products_lbl.setStyle("color", 0xFFFFFF);`

12. Save your file.

13. Test the application (Control > Test Movie). Select **Flash** from the ComboBox instance and click Get Tip. The results should look similar to the following screen shot:

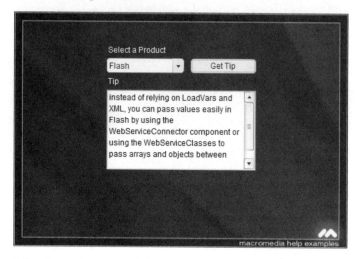

14. Select **Dreamweaver** and click Get Tip again to view another tip.

Data Integration: Using XML for a Timesheet (Flash Professional Only)

25

This tutorial shows you how to create an application for editing timesheet data. The timesheet data is stored as XML within a native XML database. The XUpdateResolver component is the best choice for this type of application, because it generates XUpdate statements that can be sent to the server to update the data.

You can print this tutorial by downloading a PDF version of it from the Macromedia Flash Documentation page at www.macromedia.com/go/fl_documentation.

In this tutorial, you will complete the following tasks:

This tutorial uses a public web service and therefore requires that you have an Internet connection. In addition, the tutorial won't work in a browser because of sandbox restrictions, but will work in the Flash authoring environment or the stand-alone Flash Player.

> The use of a public web service in this tutorial does not imply that you should use one for real-world applications. In fact, Macromedia does not recommend using public web services directly from within any client-side application. For more information, see "About data connectivity and security in Flash Player" in Flash Help.

For this tutorial, you will need to the data.xml file provided in the Tutorial Assets folder. This file can be found in one of the following locations:

- In Windows, browse to *boot drive*\Program Files\ Macromedia\ Flash 8\Samples and Tutorials\Tutorial Assets\Data Integration\ Using XML for a Timesheet\data.xml.

- On the Macintosh, browse to *Macintosh HD*/Applications/ Macromedia Flash 8/Samples and Tutorials/Tutorial Assets/ Data Integration/Using XML for a Timesheet/data.xml.

> **NOTE** For demonstration purposes, you will access the XML data from your hard disk and display the `DeltaPacket` property within your screen. In the real world, the XUpdate would be sent to the server for processing.

Create the user interface

You will begin by creating a user interface, which displays the information in the XML file.

Add XMLConnector and DataSet Components

First you will add the components that will manage the data.

1. Create a new Flash document using Flash Professional 8. Make sure your computer is connected to the Internet.

2. From the Components panel, open the Data category and drag an XMLConnector component on the Stage. In the Property inspector, enter the instance name **timeInfo_con**.

3. In the Component inspector or the Property inspector, click the Parameters tab. For the URL parameter, enter **data.xml**, and for the `Direction` parameter, select Receive from the pop-up menu.

4. From the Components panel, drag a DataSet component on the Stage. In the Property inspector, enter the instance name **timeInfo_ds**.

5. On the Stage, select the XMLConnector component. In the Component inspector, click the Schema tab. Select the `results:XML` property, and then click Import a Schema from a Sample XML File on the upper-right side of the Schema tab.

NOTE   Alternatively, you can select Import XML Schema from the Component inspector title bar menu.

6. Browse to where you saved the data.xml file, and select the file.

   The Schema tab now shows the structure of the data in the file. The `row` node is mapped to an ActionScript array of anonymous objects, because it repeats several times within the XML file. Any subnodes or attributes directly under the row node are considered properties of the anonymous objects contained within the array.

   For more information about how Flash translates XML documents into an internal schema representation, see "Data Integration (Flash Professional Only)" in Flash Help.

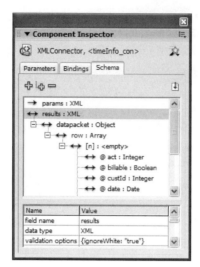

The XMLConnector component stores information internally as strings. When a request is made for the data through a DataBinding component, you can define how the string data is converted into the correct ActionScript types. This is accomplished by selecting an item within the Schema Tree pane and modifying its settings.

7. Select the Date schema field. Its type is set to String. This is because the Flash authoring tool cannot determine that it is a date type based on its value. You need to give Flash some additional information to encode this value correctly.

8. Select the Data Type parameter for the Date schema field and change it to Date. This tells the DataBinding component to try to work with this value as a date.

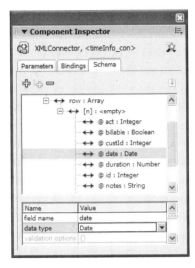

For more information on data binding and data types, see "About handling data types in data binding (Flash Professional only)" in Flash Help.

9. Select the encoder parameter for the Date schema field and change it to Date. Select the `encoder options` parameter and select the value "MM/DD/YYYY". This tells the DataBinding component how the string value is represented in the XML file. With this information, the DataBinding component can successfully take any string in this format and convert it into an ActionScript date object.

For more information on data binding and encoders, see "Schema encoders" in Flash Help.

10. Select the @billable schema field.

    The field's data type was automatically set to Boolean by the authoring tool, which looks for certain patterns to guess the type of an XML element. However, you need to modify the encoder options for the field. For Boolean data types, the encoder options specify strings that indicate true and false values.

11. With the @billable schema field still selected, double-click the Encoder Options field.

12. In the Boolean Encoder dialog box that appears, enter **true** in the Strings That Mean True text box and enter **false** in the Strings That Mean False text box.

13. Select the @duration schema field.

    The field's data type was automatically set to Integer. This is because the sample XML field contained only whole number values for this attribute.

14. Select the Data Type setting for the @duration schema field and change it to Number so that it is not limited to integer values.

15. In the Component inspector, click the Bindings tab.

16. Click the Add Binding button.

17. In the Add Binding dialog box, select the row: Array item and click OK.

18. In the Component inspector, select the Direction property and set it to Out.

19. Double-click the Bound To property.

20. In the Bound To dialog box, click the Data Set component, and then select the dataProvider: Array schema location and click OK.

The DataBinding component copies each object within the `row` array into a new record (transfer object) within the DataSet component. It applies the settings you selected as the data is copied so that the DataSet component receives ActionScript Date, Boolean, and Number fields for the `@date`, `@billable`, and `@duration` attributes.

Next, you will create fields for the DataSet component that match those in the XMLConnector component.

21. On the Stage, select the DataSet component. In the Component inspector, click the Schema tab.

22. Click Add a Component Property (+) and enter **id** for Field Name and **Integer** for Data Type.

23. Using the same method, create the following new fields:

- Field Name = **billable**, Data Type = **Boolean**
- Field Name = **date**, Data Type = **Date**
- Field Name = **duration**, Data Type = **Number**
- Field Name = **rate**, Data Type = **Number**

> **NOTE**
>
> The field names must exactly match the names of their corresponding properties within the XMLConnector component (@date = `date`, @billable = `billable`, @duration = `duration`), including capitalization.

24. Select the Date field that you just created. Select the encoder setting and change it to DateToNumber.

> **NOTE**
>
> The DataSet component needs to store date values internally in their numeric format so that they can be sorted correctly. The DateToNumber encoder converts a date into a number whenever the value is set. It converts a number into a date whenever the value is accessed.

25. With the Date field still selected, double-click the Formatter field in the Component inspector and select Date from the pop-up menu.

26. Double-click the Formatter Options field in the Component inspector.

27. In the Date Formatter Settings dialog box that appears, enter **MM-DD-YYYY** in the Format text box.

Add DataGrid and Button components

Next you will add components for displaying the data.

1. From the Components panel, open the User Interface category and drag a DataGrid component to the Stage.

2. In the Property inspector enter the instance name **timeInfo_grd**.

3. Still in the Property inspector, set the Width to **360**.

4. In the Component inspector, click the Bindings tab.

5. Click the Add Binding button.

6. In the Add Binding dialog box, select the dataProvider: Array item and click OK.

7. In the Bindings tab, click the Bound To property.

8. In the Bound To dialog box, click the Data Set component, and then select the dataProvider: Array schema location and click OK.

9. In the Bindings tab, set the Direction to In.

10. With the Data Grid still selected, go to the Component inspector Bindings tab and click the Add Binding button.

11. In the Add Binding dialog box, select the selectedIndex: Number item and click OK.

12. Double-click the Bound To property.

13. In the Bound To dialog box, click the Data Set component, and then select the selectedIndex: Number schema location and click OK.

14. Leave the Direction property set to In/Out.

15. Drag a Button component to the Stage, and give it the instance name **loadData_btn** in the Property inspector.

16. In the Component inspector, click the Parameters tab. In the Label field, type **Load Data**.

17. With the button still selected on the Stage, open the Behaviors panel (Window > Behaviors).

18. Click Add Behavior (+), and select Data > Trigger Data Source. In the Trigger Data Source dialog box, select the timeInfo_con component, and click OK.

19. Save the file in the same folder where the data.xml file resides.

20. Run the application, and click Load Data.

The XML data is retrieved, converted, and loaded into the DataSet component. The binding between the DataSet and the DataGrid copies the data into the grid for display.

Edit the data

Now you will modify the application so that you can edit data through the DataGrid component.

1. On the Stage, select the DataGrid component. Then click the Parameters tab in the Component inspector.

2. Set the `editable` property to `true`.

3. Run the application.

   You can now edit the data within the grid.

Data Integration: Using XUpdate to Update the Timesheet (Flash Professional Only)

26

Prerequisite: "Data Integration: Using XML for a Timesheet (Flash Professional Only)"

This tutorial starts where the "Data Integration: Using XML for a Timesheet (Flash Professional Only)" tutorial left off. Now that the DataSet component is managing the data, it is tracking changes that are made to the data into the `DeltaPacket` property. A resolver is needed to send the changes back to the server in an optimized way. The XUpdateResolver component is the best choice for updating an XML source, because it generates XUpdate statements that can be sent to the server to update the data.

You can print this tutorial by downloading a PDF version of it from the Macromedia Flash Documentation page at www.macromedia.com/go/fl_documentation.

In this tutorial, you will complete the following task:

This tutorial uses a public web service and therefore requires that you have an Internet connection. In addition, the tutorial won't work in a browser because of sandbox restrictions, but will work in the Flash authoring environment or Flash Player.

> **NOTE**
>
> The use of a public web service in this tutorial does not imply that you should use one for real-world applications. In fact, Macromedia does not recommend using public web services directly from within any client-side application. For more information, see "About data connectivity and security in Flash Player" in Flash Help.

For this tutorial, you will need to the data.xml file provided in the Tutorial Assets folder. This file can be found in one of the following locations:

- In Windows, browse to *boot drive*\Program Files\Macromedia\ Flash 8\Samples and Tutorials\Tutorial Assets\Data Integration\ Using XML for a Timesheet\data.xml.

- On the Macintosh, browse to *Macintosh HD*/Applications/ Macromedia Flash 8/Samples and Tutorials/Tutorial Assets/ Data Integration/Using XML for a Timesheet/data.xml.

> **NOTE**
> For demonstration purposes, you will access the XML data from your hard disk and display the `DeltaPacket` property within your screen. In the real world, the XUpdate would be sent to the server for processing.

Update the timesheet

Now you will set up the bindings to allow the timesheet to be updated.

1. Begin with the file you created in the "Data Integration: Using XML for a Timesheet (Flash Professional Only)" tutorial.

2. In the Components panel, open the Data category and drag an XUpdateResolver component to the Stage.

3. In the Property inspector, enter the instance name **timeInfo_rs**.

4. Click the Schema tab in the Component inspector, and select the `deltaPacket` component property within the Schema Tree pane.

5. Change the DeltaPacket component's encoder setting to DataSetDeltaToXUpdateDelta.

    This encoder converts data within the DeltaPacket into XPath statements that are supplied to the XUpdateResolver component, but it needs additional information from you to do its job.

6. Double-click the `encoder options` property. When prompted for a value for the `rowNodeKey` property, type **datapacket/row[@id='?id']**.

   This property identifies which node within the XML file will be treated as a record within the data set. It also defines which element or attribute combination makes the row node unique, as well as the schema field within the DataSet component that will represent it. See "Updates sent to an external data source" in Flash Help.

   In the sample XML file, the `id` attribute of the `datapacket/row` node is the unique identifier, and it will be mapped to the DataSet component's ID schema field. This is defined with the following expression:

   `datapacket/row[@id='?id']`

7. In the Component inspector, click the Bindings tab.

8. Click the Add Binding button.

9. In the Add Binding dialog box, click the `deltaPacket` property and click OK.

10. In the Component inspector Bindings tab, double-click the Bound To property.

11. In the Bound To dialog box, click the Data Set component, and then click the `deltaPacket` schema location and click OK.

    This binding will copy the DeltaPacket component to the XUpdateResolver component so that it can be manipulated before it is sent to the server.

> **NOTE** The data is copied after the DataSet component's `applyUpdates()` method is called.

12. Drag a TextArea component onto the Stage, and in the Property inspector enter the instance name **deltaText**.

13. Still in the Property inspector, set the Width to **360**.

14. Select the component, and then in the Component inspector, click the Bindings tab.

15. Click the Add Binding button.

16. In the Add Binding dialog box, click the `text: String` property and click OK.

17. In the Bindings tab, double-click the Bound To property.

18. In the Bound To dialog box, click the XUpdateResolver component, and then click the `xupdatePacket` schema location and click OK.

The update packet contains the modified version of the DeltaPacket that will be sent to the server.

19. In the Components panel, open the User Interface category and drag a Button component onto the Stage.

20. In the Property inspector, enter the instance name **btn_show**. In the Component inspector, click the Parameters tab and change the label to Show Updates.

21. With the button selected, open the Actions panel (F9) and enter the following code:

```
on (click) {
  _parent.timeInfo_ds.applyUpdates();
}
```

22. Test the application (Control > Test Movie). Load the data and make a change to one or more fields in multiple records.

23. Click Show Updates. Review the XML packet in the TextArea component.

24. Try setting the `includeDeltaPacketInfo` parameter of the XUpdateResolver component to `true` using the Component inspector.

TIP

You can copy the XML data into your favorite XML editor to make it easier to read.

NOTE

Additional information is added to the update packet. This information can be used by the server to uniquely identify this update operation. With this information, the server can generate a result packet that can be used by the XUpdateResolver component and the DataSet component to update the client data with changes from the server.

Training from the Source

Macromedia's *Training from the Source* series is one of the best-selling series on the market. This series offers you a unique self-paced approach that introduces you to the major features of the software and guides you step by step through the development of real-world projects.

Each book is divided into a series of lessons. Each lesson begins with an overview of the lesson's content and learning objectives and is divided into short tasks that break the skills into bite-size units. All the files you need for the lessons are included on the CD that comes with the book.

Macromedia Flash 8: Training from the Source
ISBN 0-321-33629-1

Macromedia Flash Professional 8: Training from the Source
ISBN 0-321-38403-2

Macromedia Flash 8 ActionScript: Training from the Source
ISBN 0-321-33619-4

Macromedia Studio 8: Training from the Source
ISBN 0-321-33620-8

Macromedia Dreamweaver 8: Training from the Source
ISBN 0-321-33626-7

Macromedia Dreamweaver 8 with ASP, PHP and ColdFusion: Training from the Source
ISBN 0-321-33625-9

Macromedia Fireworks 8: Training from the Source
ISBN 0-321-33591-0

macromedia®
PRESS

www.macromediapress.com